EDUCATION POLICY ANALYSIS

2002

ORGANISATION FOR ECONOMIC CO-OPERATION AND DEVELOPMENT

The *Education Policy Analysis* series forms part of the work programme of the OECD Education Committee and the OECD Directorate for Education. It is a collaborative effort between OECD governments, the national experts and institutions working with the OECD, and the OECD Secretariat. The series is prepared by the Education and Training Policy Division under the direction of Abrar Hasan, but draws on a range of activities in the Directorate. The principal contributions to the 2002 issue were made by Phillip McKenzie and Donald Hirsch as editors, John Bennett (Chapter 1), Andreas Schleicher (Chapter 2), Paulo Santiago (Chapter 3), Kurt Larsen and Stéphan Vincent-Lancrin (Chapter 4), and Simon Field (Chapter 5). Sophie Vayssettes and Hannah Cocks provided statistical support. Copy editing was the responsibility of Marlène Mohier and Delphine Grandrieux. Fung-Kwan Tam was responsible for graphic design. Noeleen El Hachem was responsible for administration. Colleagues in the OECD Secretariat provided helpful comments on initial drafts. Valuable comments on draft chapters were provided by national representatives of the OECD Education Committee, members of the Governing Board of the Centre for Educational Research and Innovation (CERI), national co-ordinators of the Indicators of National Education Systems (INES) project, and their colleagues. The views expressed in the published chapters, however, do not necessarily represent those of OECD Member governments.

ORGANISATION FOR ECONOMIC CO-OPERATION AND DEVELOPMENT

Pursuant to Article 1 of the Convention signed in Paris on 14th December 1960, and which came into force on 30th September 1961, the Organisation for Economic Co-operation and Development (OECD) shall promote policies designed:

- to achieve the highest sustainable economic growth and employment and a rising standard of living in Member countries, while maintaining financial stability, and thus to contribute to the development of the world economy;
- to contribute to sound economic expansion in Member as well as non-member countries in the process of economic development; and
- to contribute to the expansion of world trade on a multilateral, non-discriminatory basis in accordance with international obligations.

The original Member countries of the OECD are Austria, Belgium, Canada, Denmark, France, Germany, Greece, Iceland, Ireland, Italy, Luxembourg, the Netherlands, Norway, Portugal, Spain, Sweden, Switzerland, Turkey, the United Kingdom and the United States. The following countries became Members subsequently through accession at the dates indicated hereafter: Japan (28th April 1964), Finland (28th January 1969), Australia (7th June 1971), New Zealand (29th May 1973), Mexico (18th May 1994), the Czech Republic (21st December 1995), Hungary (7th May 1996), Poland (22nd November 1996), Korea (12th December 1996) and Slovak Republic (14th December 2000). The Commission of the European Communities takes part in the work of the OECD (Article 13 of the OECD Convention).

The Centre for Educational Research and Innovation was created in June 1968 by the Council of the Organisation for Economic Co-operation and Development and all Member countries of the OECD are participants.

The main objectives of the Centre are as follows:

- *analyse and develop research, innovation and key indicators in current and emerging education and learning issues, and their links to other sectors of policy;*
- *explore forward-looking coherent approaches to education and learning in the context of national and international cultural, social and economic change; and*
- *facilitate practical co-operation among Member countries and, where relevant, with non-member countries, in order to seek solutions and exchange views of educational problems of common interest.*

The Centre functions within the Organisation for Economic Co-operation and Development in accordance with the decisions of the Council of the Organisation, under the authority of the Secretary-General. It is supervised by a Governing Board composed of one national expert in its field of competence from each of the countries participating in its programme of work.

Publié en français sous le titre :
Analyse des politiques d'éducation
ÉDITION 2002

TABLE OF CONTENTS

LIST OF BOXES, FIGURES AND TABLES

BOXES

FIGURES

INTRODUCTION

In 2001 OECD Education Ministers endorsed the theme of *investing in competencies for all* to guide the education work of the Organisation over the next five years. This theme reflects the goal of ensuring that all citizens have the basic competencies on which other learning depends, and the high-level intellectual and social competencies necessary for full engagement in the knowledge society. It builds on the commitments Ministers made to *lifelong learning for all* in 1996.

Education policy increasingly embraces the entire spectrum of learning: from the pre-school years, through primary and secondary schooling and tertiary education to adult learning. Education must build strong foundations for learning; and also enable people to continue building by developing the motivation and competence to manage their own learning. The education policy agenda is both long-term and multi-faceted. Its very breadth can raise concerns about where priorities should be placed, and how effective new strategies can be introduced. The analyses reported annually in *Education Policy Analysis* are intended to assist in these deliberations.

It is increasingly recognised that high-quality programmes are needed to give all young children a strong start in lifelong learning. An unequal start in learning will become increasingly costly to remedy later on, as well as individually damaging and socially divisive. And yet, in a number of countries policy making and programme coverage in the early childhood area remains fragmented and piecemeal. Chapter 1 draws on country experience and recent research to provide a better understanding of how the pieces can be put together more coherently.

The OECD is also improving the evidence base on school-level policies that provide a strong foundation for lifelong learning. For example, the Programme for International Student Assessment (PISA) indicated that there is substantial variation among countries, and within some countries, in 15 year-olds' achievement in reading, mathematical and scientific literacy. However, the further analyses of PISA reported in Chapter 2 show that it is possible to combine high performance standards with an equitable distribution of learning outcomes. Quality and equity need not be seen as competing policy objectives.

In identifying the need for schools to adapt to changing social circumstances, and to successfully meet the learning requirements of all young people, OECD Education Ministers have placed a strong emphasis on the capacity of the teaching workforce. However, there are serious difficulties in many countries in maintaining an adequate supply of good quality teachers, and further developing the skills of those already in the profession. Chapter 3 argues that teacher shortages raise concerns about quality as well as quantity. It reviews the international data on measures of shortfalls in teacher supply, identifies the policy challenges that shortages give rise to, and outlines policy tools that need to be considered.

One interesting means by which increasing numbers of students manage their own learning is by travelling to another country to study, or by accessing overseas education services while living at home. Rapid developments in e-learning, and competition from a wide range of education and training providers, are accelerating these trends. While data on such developments remain uneven, Chapter 4 provides a major new profile of cross-border education activity. The increased connectivity among national education systems means that difficult policy questions about student access, institutional funding and regulation, and quality assurance, now need to be confronted in an international context.

People's motivation to learn and competence to manage their learning is fundamental to promoting lifelong learning. The importance of strengthening these aspects is brought out in Chapter 5. It draws on recent empirical work to argue that the concept of "human capital" needs to be broadened beyond directly productive capacities to encompass the characteristics that allow a person to build, manage and deploy his/her skills. These include the ability and motivation to learn, effective job search skills, and personal characteristics that help one work well, as well as the capacity to blend a successful life with a good career. Such competencies, which are critical for economic success as well as social and personal development, need to be more explicitly built into educational policies and programmes.

To assist Member countries in such important tasks, the OECD is giving education a higher profile in its work. On 1 September 2002 a new Directorate for Education was created. As the OECD Secretary-General said, "our work on education will retain important connections with our work in other areas such as employment, social issues, science and technology, governance, and macro-economics but its independent status makes clear the importance we attach to it". This higher profile reflects the greater emphasis that Member countries are placing on education, and developing people's competencies more generally. A well-educated population that is engaged in on-going learning is fundamental to social and economic development, as well as an important goal in its own right.

chapter 1

STRENGTHENING EARLY CHILDHOOD PROGRAMMES: A POLICY FRAMEWORK

▼

SUMMARY

High-quality early childhood programmes give young children a strong start in lifelong learning. When made accessible to all, they also help strengthen social equity. This chapter draws on country experience and recent research to identify eight key strategies for improving access to quality early childhood education and care (ECEC):

– A *systemic approach to child policy*, co-ordinated across ministries and across layers of government. This helps deploy resources more efficiently and provide coherent services.

– A *strong and equal partnership with education*, which enables shared goals and approaches to be developed.

– A *universal approach to access*, both by extending free places to over-threes and by developing under-threes provision, especially for children with special needs.

– *Substantial public investment*, requiring consideration of how resources are deployed and costs are shared between governments and families.

– *Quality improvement and assurance* more consistently addressed by governments, related both to child development and societal goals.

– *Appropriate training and working conditions*, more evenly applied, in order to recruit and develop a quality workforce in sufficient numbers.

– *Evaluation, monitoring and data collection* that is more systematic, and pays attention to outcomes.

– *Research and evaluation* designed to inform the long-term development of ECEC.

In countries committed to improving their early childhood services, an overarching concern is to resolve the tensions between expanding access, maintaining equity and affordability, and ensuring high quality programmes. This chapter looks at how these eight strategies may be implemented, and the tensions between competing objectives resolved.

INTRODUCTION: EIGHT KEY STRATEGIES

In its recent review of early childhood policy in twelve countries (see Box 1.1), the OECD identified eight policy strategies that help to promote equitable access to high-quality early childhood service provision. These strategies are closely inter-related. They do not entail a tightly prescriptive or standardised approach, but allow room for indi-vidual countries, systems and services to interpret them in different ways. They are, in summary:

– A systemic approach to policy development and integration;

– A strong and equal partnership with the educa-tion system;

– A universal approach to access, with particular attention to children in need of special support;

– Substantial public investment in services and infrastructure;

– A participatory approach to quality improve-ment and assurance;

– Appropriate training and working conditions for staff in all forms of provision;

– Attention to evaluation, monitoring and data collection; and

– A framework and long-term agenda for research and evaluation.

This chapter follows up the OECD's major report on early childhood and care (OECD, 2001a) to analyse more precisely how these eight strategies can be pursued. It draws on recent country experience and research findings to discuss their implementation in a range of different settings.

1. A SYSTEMIC APPROACH TO POLICY DEVELOPMENT AND IMPLEMENTATION

Across countries, as policy makers seek to improve the continuity of children's early childhood experiences and make the most efficient use of resources, a systemic and integrated approach to early childhood services is gaining ground. The advantages are considerable. Adopting a more integrated approach to the field allows governments to organise common policies, and combine resources for early childhood services. Regulatory, funding and staffing regimes, costs to parents, and opening hours can be made more consistent. Variations in access and quality can be lessened, and links at the services level – across age groups and settings – are more easily created. In integrated systems, a common vision of education and care can be forged, with agreed social and pedagogical objectives.

A common understanding of how care and educa-tion can contribute together to children's develop-ment and learning has not been reached in all countries. For historical reasons, policies for the

---

Box 1.1 **The OECD thematic review of early childhood education and care policy**

In March 1998, the OECD launched a series of country reviews of early childhood education and care (ECEC) policy. The rationale was both practical and urgent: because of changing labour market profiles, the provision of early childhood services had become necessary in most countries if young children were to be adequately cared for, and women with young children were to have choice and equality of opportunity in the workplace. Research also pointed to the value of high-quality ECEC experiences in promoting the cognitive, social and emotional well-being of children, and later, their long-term success in school and life.

Twelve countries participated: Australia, Belgium, the Czech Republic, Denmark, Finland, Italy, the Netherlands, Norway, Portugal, Sweden, the United Kingdom and the United States. Between 1998 and 2000, the countries prepared background reports and hosted visits by OECD reviewers. The results were discussed in the comparative report, *Starting Strong: Early Childhood Education and Care* (OECD, 2001a). A further round of reviews covering other countries will take place from 2002 to 2004. Information on the visits and reports is available at *www.oecd.org/els/education/earlychildhood*

"care" and "education" of young children have often developed separately, with different systems of governance, funding streams and training for staff. Responsibility for early childhood services is sometimes divided among several ministries, based more on traditional divisions of government than on the needs of families and young children today. In addition, the trend towards decentralisation has led in some countries to a weakening of central policy making for the field, and to a diversification of services to meet local needs and preferences. In sum, problems of policy co-ordination occur across ministries ("horizontal" co-ordination) and between different levels of government ("vertical" co-ordination).

1.1 Co-ordination across ministries

Administrative integration, that is, shifting national responsibility for ECEC to one lead ministry, is becoming a preferred means of integrating policy at the national level. It is the solution adopted for example by Denmark, Finland, Norway and Sweden, and allows immediate integration at the level dealing with the framing of legislation, major policy orientations and regulatory steering. Sweden is the only country reviewed that has fully integrated all early childhood services and the compulsory schools under the Ministry of Education, but there are signs that other countries may follow this model. Yet, it seems to matter less whether the lead ministry is education, social welfare, or family affairs, than to acknowledge that the education, care and social functions of early childhood services are part of a comprehensive policy, with an integrated approach to goal setting, financing, staffing and monitoring. Another advantage of administrative and conceptual integration of ECEC policy is that it can address the needs of children under the age of three, which in many countries have not been given the policy priority necessary to ensure adequate quality and access.

Having a lead ministry, however, does not remove the need for co-ordination across departments at a senior management level. Early childhood policy is not only a matter of providing education and care to young children, but is also strongly linked with the provision of paid maternity and parental leave, family support, health, social and employment policies. One option is the creation

of an inter-departmental co-ordination body. In Denmark, for example, an Inter-Ministerial Committee on Children was set up in 1987 as an interdisciplinary body of the various ministries with responsibility for matters relating to children and families. Chaired by the Ministry of Social Affairs, the Committee's main objective is to create coherence relating to children and families, and to promote cross-sectoral initiatives.

1.2 Co-ordination across layers of government

In most countries, ECEC policy and provision is a shared responsibility between national and local governments. Generally, a national government's use of discretionary funding gives it a powerful steering mechanism which can be used to ensure that local authorities and groups pursue national goals and deliver agreed outcomes. However, effective decentralisation also needs to be based on the principle of collaborative relationships between the centre and the local actors. In countries with dynamic ECEC sectors, governments not only ensure that national objectives are understood, but also give appropriate support to local authorities and help to build up local management expertise.

Within local authorities, there is also an issue of integration of services. Many have brought together children's services and education portfolios to facilitate coherence and co-ordination for young children. In the Nordic countries, local authorities generally have full responsibility for programme management, design and quality, albeit governed by national guidelines and shared with professional staff and parent groups. Box 1.2 describes Dutch initiatives in policy co-ordination.

2. A STRONG AND EQUAL PARTNERSHIP WITH THE EDUCATION SYSTEM

Historically, "childcare" has often had little to do with "education", especially where the emphasis has been on social welfare or caring for a small minority of children while their parents worked. These features of the care sector are changing radically today, as increasing numbers of young children from all backgrounds need early childhood services. Conscious of this change, the OECD review teams underlined that a strong partner-

---

Box 1.2   A Dutch example of policy co-ordination

Starting from a relatively low base of provision in the early 1990s, the Netherlands is moving towards an integrated framework of services for young children aged from 0-6 years that crosses traditional ministerial lines, and is achieving consensus with local authorities about policy goals. ECEC policy and provision has become a shared responsibility between national, provincial and local governments:

• At central government level, two ministries have major responsibility for young children. The Ministry of Health, Welfare and Sport (VWS) has responsibility for family support, socio-educational activities and the funding and supervision of out-of-home care. The Ministry of Education, Culture and Science (OCenW) is responsible for children in primary education from 4 years upwards.

• A national framework was created in 1998 to give direction to local policy planners at the same time that Educational Priority Areas were decentralised to the municipalities. The stated goal was to improve the starting conditions of children at the beginning of primary school, by increasing co-operation between local schools, playgroups and childcare centres. By linking the funding transfers to certain conditions at the local level, the framework agreement encouraged municipalities to: a) exchange information concerning pupils entering primary schools; b) promote systematic planning in pre-school provision; and c) whenever necessary, implement strategies that foster pre-school language development and provide support to parents.

---

ship between early childhood and the education ministries can have a number of advantages, notably:

– To ensure recognition of ECEC as part of mainstream public provision;

– To create shared goals for early childhood programmes;

– To underline the specific goals and educational methods of early childhood services; and

– To organise in a coherent manner the recruitment, training and career structures of staff in both sectors.

2.1 The link with education brings broad public recognition

In many countries, early childhood professionals fear that an over-emphasis on "education" will create a school-like approach to the organisation of early childhood provision. Yet, if the specificity of quality early childhood services can be maintained,

there are important advantages to be gained from working alongside education.

A first advantage is the recognition of ECEC as part of mainstream public provision. When the developmental and educational benefits of early childhood services are recognised, they become entitled to regular public financing and, in parallel, more systematic approaches to child learning, programme development, and issues such as staff training and work conditions are adopted. More recently too, the issue of successful transitions of children from early childhood services into primary school has become a subject of common interest to both sectors, and much innovative cross-sectoral work is taking place (National Center for Early Development and Learning, 2000; Dockett and Perry, 2001). Within this framework of co-operation, the particular goals, learning theory and pedagogical methods of ECEC services are better understood, and are now acquiring a more secure place in universities and training colleges.

2.2 Partnership can bring greater agreement about ECEC programme objectives

In Section 1, we outlined how an integrated approach across all ministries toward goal setting, financing, staffing and monitoring leads to more *efficient* policy making for young children. The experience of the OECD review also suggests that partnership between the responsible ministries – and/or municipal authorities – brings a clearer understanding of the social, care and education functions of early childhood provision, and can lead to more *effective* programmes that support the holistic development and learning of children. A challenge in some national systems is that, on the one hand, programmes for the youngest children can be insufficiently educational while, on the other, pre-school programmes within educational settings can be over-didactic, and fail to support sufficiently the general well-being and socio-emotional needs of young children. Co-operation between the ministries responsible for children's programmes can bring greater agreement about programme objectives and methodologies.

Across countries, the following objectives for early childhood centres are encountered:

– To create secure, caring and enriched environments which foster children's overall development and well-being;

– To enhance school readiness and children's later educational outcomes; and

– To support children at risk of school failure through enriched programmes and an early introduction to a common language and culture.

In the United States, the National Education Goals Panel (1997) identified five dimensions that contribute to the child's development and later success in school, namely: health and physical development; emotional well-being and social competence; positive approaches to learning; communication skills; and cognition and general knowledge. For children living in poor neighbourhoods and at-risk conditions, social and cultural inclusion is also a crucial goal, which makes parental involvement and support necessary. Projects to promote inclusion also commonly involve child welfare, health, housing, job training and other social agencies. Quality early childhood programmes will generally take account of these various dimensions and, where necessary, create partnerships with local agencies.

In their approaches to the youngest children, many countries now encourage the employment of educational staff and the use of developmental curricula. Children in crèches and early services are offered enriched learning environments in which they can explore, play and enjoy positive social interaction, both with caregivers and other children. In well-structured programmes, a wide range of arts, crafts, co-operative games and activities are also provided. In countries where the presence of well-trained personnel is combined with favourable child-staff ratios, staff are able to give close attention to each child, so as to extend emergent strengths, understandings and skills.

Such elements are found also in programmes for the older (4-6 years) children, but with an additional emphasis in most countries on structured *learning areas* – in particular, nature and the environment, emergent literacy, numeracy, general knowledge, scientific concepts and reasoning (EUROSTAT, 2000). These learning areas are most often presented in detail in curricula, and again receive most focus when teacher assessments at entry into primary school are used. Recent research on early learning points to the benefits of consciously guiding children toward such culturally valued activities, and to using an approach to learning that includes both child-initiated activities and teacher instruction (Bowman *et al.*, 2000). According to Leseman (2002), recent neuro-science research supports the view that to achieve the best and most enduring results in early childhood programmes, both cognitive and socio-emotional outcomes should be pursued simultaneously. Children's self-esteem, self-confidence, work attitudes and social skills support cognitive development, while, in turn, cognitive achievement reinforces the well-being and self-image of children.

In the pre-school classes, how are the more formal learning areas introduced to children? In general, well-trained professionals lead young children into the learning areas through both structured activities and play. Structured programmes provide security for children and ensure that the key concepts and skills involved in important learning areas are thoroughly understood and mastered. While direct instruction and explanation may be used – along with a broad variety of other pedagogical techniques – such programmes do not have to be rigidly didactic. For example, in Finland, spontaneity, space and choice are offered to children – even into the early classes of primary education – within structured activities in which the particular interests and initiatives of the individual child are taken into account. Throughout the day and in all aspects of the centre's life, whether it is at meal times or in a literacy activity, teachers can support children through modelling, encouragement and guidance. Respectful of the child's interest, they create with children challenging learning experiences that extend the child's capabilities and symbolic abilities. As in the project work in the Reggio Emilia schools in Italy, staff can encourage children to reflect, question and hypothesise, and to be responsible for their work and for each other (Edwards *et al.*, 1996).

In the Nordic countries – and in many model programmes all over the world – emphasis is placed also on childhood as a unique stage in its own right, and on supporting development both on the child's own terms and in relation to communal and social values. While learning is stressed – including in many centres, support for emergent literacy activities – experienced educational advisors in these countries note that an emphasis on the child's own interests, on interactive group work and on child-initiated activities develops children's self-esteem, social responsibility and inter-personal skills. Programmes are generally characterised by a child-centred approach, the pursuit of broad developmental goals, programmatic diversity, favourable child-staff ratios (allowing individualised attention and interaction) and staff who are well-trained in early childhood methodology. A broad view of intellectual development is adopted (see Gardner, 2000), and children are encouraged to develop multiple intelligences in their play and small group activities. Physical space is arranged to allow for children's free choice and exploration rather than channelling children and teachers by necessity toward whole group activities.

In the English- and French-speaking countries, programmes for young children are generally more aca-demic, and tend to focus on cognitive development, and on early literacy and numeracy. The greater heterogeneity of populations in these countries may explain this approach, as in many early childhood centres there may be a high proportion of bilingual children, and of children at-risk of school failure. In such a context, an emphasis on language and school readiness is understandable, although limitations of space, especially in urban areas, may also be a factor inhibiting more exploratory processes. In the early childhood centres in these countries, much evidence of literacy activity can be seen. Teacher-initiated and large group activities may predominate, and a "language hour" may be scheduled each day. In the best centres, however, teachers are well aware that learning must be enjoyable for children, and should build on children's existing understanding and interests. Many of the pedagogical activities take place, in fact, within a context of play. In such centres, *e.g.* in the Early Excellence Centres in England, a much less constraining use of space is practised than, for example, in the traditional reception classes.

Research suggests that, in their best manifestations, both the developmental and balanced instruction approaches are valid, if developmental and pedagogical goals are included in each, and the developmental rhythms of children are respected. A conclusion drawn by Leseman *et al.* (1998) in their statistical meta-analysis of major evaluation studies of centre-based pre-school programmes, is that, once sufficient duration and intensity of programmes are ensured, positive and long-lasting outcomes in both the cognitive and socio-emotional domains are most likely to be delivered by structured programmes with clear developmental and pedagogical aims. These effects are further reinforced by favourable child-staff ratios, and by the presence of sufficient numbers of well-trained staff using a range of pedagogical approaches and materials adapted to the strengths and needs of the children (Bowman *et al.*, 2000).

3. A UNIVERSAL APPROACH TO ACCESS

As Figure 1.1 shows, participation in ECEC varies significantly among OECD countries. In considering how to widen access, countries have often looked at the age at which all children are in

STRENGTHENING EARLY CHILDHOOD PROGRAMMES:
A POLICY FRAMEWORK

Figure 1.1 Net enrolment rates by single year of age in pre-primary[1] and primary education, 2000 (%)

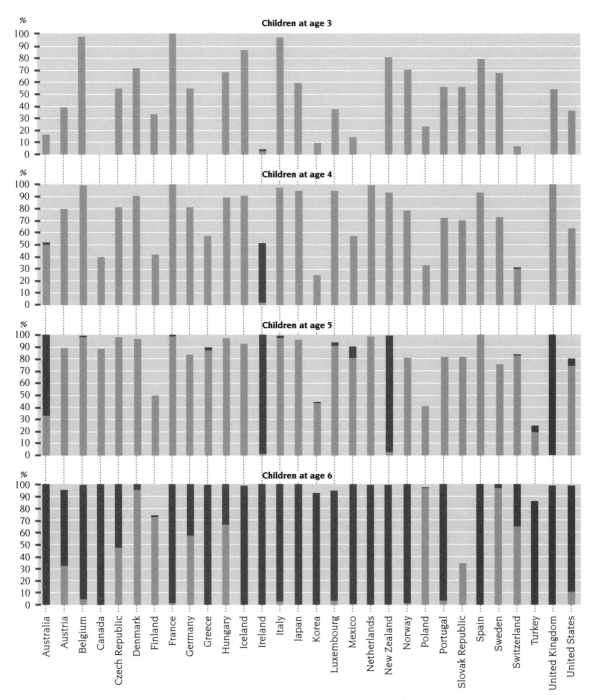

1. The data refer to pre-primary education, which is limited to organised centre-based programmes designed to foster learning and emotional and social development in children from 3 to compulsory school age. Day care, play groups and home-based structured and developmental activities may not be included in these data. In some countries, the net enrolment rate at age 6 exceeds 100% due to different reference dates for counting enrolments in various programmes.

Source: OECD (2002).

Data for Figure 1.1, p. 34.

principle guaranteed a free place in early childhood education and care – generally some time between the ages of 3 and 6. In fact, access has a number of other dimensions: *scope of access* (does provision, whether free or charging fees, meet the needs of parents for under-three provision, for out-of school care, for care in special circumstances?); *location of services* (is provision convenient for families, including families in rural areas and travelling families?); *needs of children* (in terms of equitable and appropriate access for children requiring special support); and *ability to pay* (ensuring that fees are affordable).

3.1 Free, universal access for all 3- to 6-year-olds

The age at which young children have a legal right to attend free, school-based early childhood education and care varies considerably across countries. The age is two-and-half years in Belgium, three years in Italy, and age four in the Netherlands and the United Kingdom.[1] In some other countries with weaker legal entitlements, *de facto* provision has been growing rapidly. For example, in Portugal, a significant expansion in public investment in the pre-school network meant that between 1996 and 1999, coverage increased dramatically, from 57% to 72% of children over 3 years old, and over 90% of 5-year-olds benefit from a free daily five-hour session in the *jardim de infância*. In the United States, where almost all 5-year-olds attend non-compulsory kindergarten within the formal school system, the number of part-time state-funded pre-kindergarten programmes for 3- and 4-year-olds has grown significantly (Schulman *et al.*, 1999).

3.2 Increasing provision for infants and toddlers

Relative to services for pre-school children, less attention has been given by most countries to provision for children under three years. National data on services for these children are often unsatisfactory, in part due to the variety of providers and informal arrangements for the age group, and in part due to regional or local responsibility for these services. We do know, however, that publicly subsidised services are provided primarily in centres and family day care homes, and that nearly all charge parental fees. Higher socio-economic groups tend to use these services more

than do lower socio-economic groups, particularly immigrant and ethnic minority parents. The highest levels of enrolment of under-threes in subsidised provision are seen in Denmark and Sweden,[2] countries with a long history of publicly funded ECEC as part of broader gender equity and family policies. With the exception of Finland and Sweden, reports from all review countries indicate that the demand for services is significantly higher than the available number of places, including in those countries that provide long parental leave, a measure that helps to reduce demand, especially in the first year.

Box 1.3 (overleaf) schematises the degree of support provided by countries both to out-of-home care for children under 3 years, and to parental leave to enable parents to remain at home to look after infants and young children. In countries grouped in Approach C in Box 1.3, there are signs that the concept of services for the under-threes is broadening to include objectives regarding education, gender equality, social integration, and family support. These services are considered not just as necessary support for parental employment, but as a public service that can benefit both children and parents. In Italy, for example, government proposals in 1998 described the shift in understanding of the *asilo nido* as a service on "individual demand" to "an educational and social service of public interest". As a result, flexible services for families with young children – full-time, part-time, drop-in centres and playgroups – have been developed, which support parents regardless of whether they work or not. There is also an increasing focus on the educational role of services for very young children, which is supported by research showing that the first three years of life are extremely important in setting attitudes and patterns of thinking (Shore, 1997; Shonkoff and

---

1. In Italy, pre-primary education is free only in state-run and municipal schools, not in private schools, although in general, only modest fees are required in the majority of voluntary schools. In the Netherlands, by legislation, voluntary schools are fully subsidised and cannot demand fees. The daily and annual duration of provision varies widely from country to country.

2. In Sweden, because of the long and generous parental leave scheme, infants are rarely seen in day-care services, and are normally first enrolled between the age of 15 to 18 months.

STRENGTHENING EARLY CHILDHOOD PROGRAMMES:
A POLICY FRAMEWORK

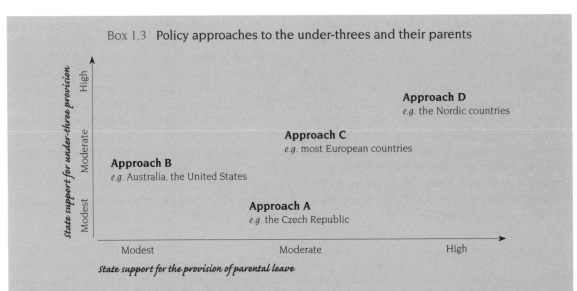

Box 1.3   Policy approaches to the under-threes and their parents

Approach A

Moderate state support for parental leave but with little or no support for under-three services. For example, the policy in the Czech Republic favours parents (meaning mothers) caring for their child until at least age three, with few publicly-supported alternatives. In 2001, there were only 67 public crèches, serving less than 1% of children, compared to 20% coverage in 1989. The question as to whether women who stay at home to rear their children (and hence forego wages and pension rights) should have the right to a more equitable compensation is not a major issue in public debate.

Approach B

Modest to moderate state support for under-three services, channelled especially toward low-income families, but with little or no support for parental leave. In Australia and the United States, there is moderate state support for under-three services, but little direct support for parental leave. Although enrolment rates in registered centres in Australia are lower than in the United States, greater financial support is given to parents to access services.

Approach C

Moderate state support to parental leave with modest to moderate support to under-three provision, especially for low-income groups. A third approach, offered in the majority of countries reviewed, is modest to moderate help from government for centre-based education and care, but families are still viewed as primarily responsible for providing or finding childcare for their children. There is a period of paid statutory parental leave (Italy, Portugal, United Kingdom), with modest levels of publicly funded services, generally insufficient to meet public demand. "Childcare" is subsidised primarily for working or disadvantaged parents. Toward the other end of the scale, Belgium (where all children are entitled to a free educational place from 2.5 years) and the Netherlands combine short periods of low-paid leave with stronger levels of public provision for the under-threes.

Approach D

Strong state support both to parents and under-three services. In this fourth model, there are two different emphases. In Finland and Norway, the main objective is parental choice supported by strong government investment in child and family services. Child-care leave or cash benefit schemes allow one parent to stay out of the workforce to care for their child until the age of between 18 months and three years, and provision for children under three is publicly subsidised. In Finland, there is a statutory right for every child to a place in a publicly subsidised service, while in Norway addressing the shortages in provision for the under-threes has become a political priority. In Denmark and Sweden, policy emphasises parental employment after a comparatively well-paid parental leave of 12 months and 18 months, respectively. A guaranteed place in a quality publicly subsidised ECEC service is generally available on a sliding-scale, fee-paying basis. Few infants attend ECEC settings *before* the end of the parental leave period.

Phillips, 2000). This new understanding is increasingly reflected in national curricula, *e.g.* in Norway and New Zealand, which make no distinction between the learning capacities of infants/toddlers and older children.

In sum, despite a very low base in many countries, provision for the under-threes is receiving greater government attention and funding, and can serve a wide range of objectives. Many governments have recently introduced policies to improve: parental leave (Italy, Norway, United Kingdom); family-friendly work practices (Netherlands, Norway); the possibility for parents to establish crèche services (Sweden, Finland); and access to early services in rural areas (*e.g.* Australia, Finland, Portugal). Strategies have also been employed to address access barriers especially for low-income families, or to address supply-side barriers in those countries where investment in services for poor neighbourhoods has not been as strong as in the Nordic countries.

3.3 Free, full and appropriate access for children with special needs

The special educational needs of children relate on the one hand, to physical, mental or sensory disabilities, and on the other, to learning difficulties deriving from socio-cultural and linguistic disadvantages. In practice, many children in need of special educational support have accumulated both physical and socio-cultural at-risk factors. Early childhood services are particularly important for such children, and contribute powerfully to their sensory-motor, emotional, social and cognitive development. Moreover, these services fulfil an early screening function in detecting special needs. Once identified, disabilities can be treated, learning difficulties foreseen and support to families offered.

When the need for special educational support arises primarily from socio-economic and socio-cultural disadvantage, early services are likewise helpful for children. The social and educational benefits are such that governments in all countries are expanding services to disadvantaged children, so as to give them the opportunity to benefit from the care and learning programmes offered in quality ECEC provision (OECD, 1999). Evaluations in several countries (*e.g.* the Netherlands, Portugal,

the United Kingdom) show, however, that when disadvantaged children participate in ECEC, they often do not receive the full range of child development, health and family services that are needed to optimise their learning (Kempson, 1996). Different types of intervention are needed, in fact, for different types of special need.

For *children with disabilities*, the policy favoured by most countries, and recommended by the UN Convention on the Rights of the Child, is inclusion in mainstream ECEC. Nordic countries give priority to such children in enrolment, and provide resources for the extra staff they require. Effective inclusion requires also appropriate organisation and management to provide premises and group sizes that meet these children's needs, as well as suitable pedagogical and curricular approaches.

For *children with special educational needs deriving from ethnic, cultural and linguistic difference*, who are often under-represented in ECEC, extra resources can help address the lack of information and language barriers that prevent the families of these children from making full use of services. They help also to provide the culturally appropriate educational materials, staff training and outreach that these families need. Australia, Belgium, the Netherlands, Norway, Portugal, Sweden (see Box 1.4 overleaf), and the United Kingdom all provide subsidies for these purposes. Provision is also made to enable parents to integrate into the host society more effectively, to enter the labour market and, in some countries, to have access to language courses. As Danish experience shows, when such approaches acknowledge and welcome cultural diversity, they are more acceptable to immigrant communities than when they are perceived as assimilatory.

For *children with special educational needs deriving from poverty and low socio-economic status*, research and practice point to the need to reduce national child poverty levels and to co-ordinate family and child policies more effectively (Morris *et al.*, 2001). At the system level, the reduction of at-risk factors in early childhood implies – as the Sure Start initiative in England illustrates – close co-operation between early childhood authorities and other ministries, so that ECEC programming, the provision of nutritional supplements, health screening, outreach to families and special financing measures become part of a single

---

Box 1.4   Rinkeby in Sweden – an intercultural approach

In Rinkeby, a district of Stockholm, 73% of residents are from immigrant backgrounds and 50 different languages are spoken by the 1 400 children attending 24 pre-schools. A multicultural project aims to allow these children to thrive in Swedish society. A single framework from age 1 to 16 aims to develop academic knowledge, language, social competence and personal maturity.

Focus on language. The project promotes the preservation of children's first language by urging families to speak it at home and employing home-language teachers, while encouraging written as well as oral language to be part of daily life. However, since children who enter school are expected to speak Swedish, pre-school is used to help children develop their competence in the Swedish language.

Partnerships with parents. Parents in Rinkeby may not be familiar with the norms and values of Swedish society. An effort is made to see parents as equals and to determine how they can contribute to the centres, which acknowledge and teach about ethnic traditions.

Links with research. Staff are in continuous contact with the Rinkeby Research Institute on Multilingual Studies. The Institute arranges joint in-service training courses for teachers in schools and pre-schools, including study of immigration, second-language acquisition and assessment of bilingual children.

Resources for staff. Rinkeby receives more public money per child than other areas of Stockholm. The city and state allocate additional funds to recruit extra staff as home-language teachers and for children in need of special support.

---

strategy. At the level of the individual centre, home links, parent groups, and collaboration with family welfare and referral agencies, are key strategies, especially when families combine a number of at-risk indicators (Sameroff and Fiese, 2000). Improved centre leadership, clear inter-cultural and integration aims, a strong pedagogical programme with a differentiated curriculum, staff development and investment in extra staff can also provide proactive support to these children, enabling, for example, the more interactive and focussed pedagogical methods which these children need (Fraser, 2002). Trained extra staff allow also an adequate response to the individual child's developmental and learning needs – a basic requirement for children with learning difficulties.

3.4 Out-of-school provision[3]

Out-of-school provision for children of working parents has not been a policy priority in most countries, yet demand for it is growing rapidly. Most school-based ECEC does not cover the full working day, and many parents – up to 30% in some countries – work non-standard hours. In addition, most school-based ECEC programmes are closed during the summer holidays and other periods when parents are working. A more coherent approach to out-of-school provision is needed, more closely linked in concept and organisation to ECEC and school provision.

Currently, Sweden and Denmark are the only countries that provide enough places – generally in early childhood centres or on school premises – to meet demand. In Sweden, all children under 12 have a legal entitlement to this form of provision. Staff engaged to look after the children are trained at higher education level. In most other countries, out-of-school provision is loosely regulated, with a range of varying services and few reliable statistics. However, recent years have seen promising national

---

3. Also known as "wrap-around care" in the context of part-day pre-school, or "school-aged childcare" for children in primary school.

Figure 1.2	Expenditure on pre-primary education as a percentage of GDP, 1999

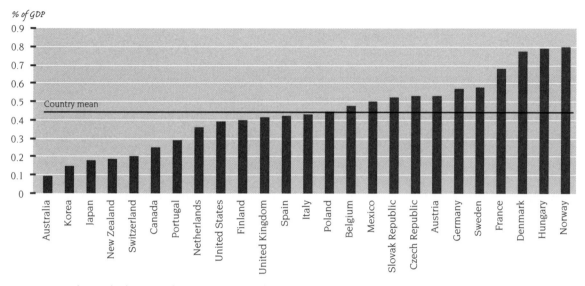

Note: Comprises direct and indirect expenditure on pre-primary educational institutions, from public and private sources.
Source: OECD (2002). ....
Data for Figure 1.2, p. 34.

initiatives. In the Netherlands, the quality regulations for ECEC in the welfare sector also apply to out-of-school provision, including staff qualifications. In Belgium, the issue of regulation is also being raised and new initiatives are taking place, *e.g.* the 2001 survey by the French Community of all leisure-time activities for children up to 12 years (Observatoire de l'Enfance, 2001). Out-of-school provision in Portugal is also being expanded, mainly in social priority areas aimed at improving the integration of marginalised groups. In the United States, Head Start[4] is implementing a major initiative to expand full-day/full-year services through partnerships with other early childhood programmes and funding sources.

4. PUBLIC INVESTMENT IN SERVICES AND INFRASTRUCTURE

Both country experience and research indicate that significant public funding is necessary to support an equitable and high-quality early childhood system, and that this spending can be justified by significant social payoffs (OECD, 2001*a*). For example, a recent study of childcare in Zurich shows that the city's public investment of CHF18 million annually is offset by CHF29 million of additional tax revenues and reduced public spending on social aid (Kucera

and Bauer, 2001). Their findings are corroborated by research from many countries and today, a strong economic rationale exists in favour of establishing national networks of early childhood services (ESO/Swedish Finance Ministry Report, 1999; Urrutia, 1999; Van der Gaag, 2002; Vandell and Wolfe, 2000; Verry, 2000). Benefits include an immediate employment gain, higher tax revenues, less social welfare dependency, and later savings in educational and social expenditure.

Figure 1.2 shows that despite the strength of the social and economic argument, and a general trend towards greater investment, spending averages less than 0.5% of GDP and is highly variable across countries. This raises three important questions.

4.1 Who pays for ECEC?

In most countries, a distinction may be drawn between services for children aged over and under

---

4. Head Start is a federally-funded programme in the US that provides comprehensive developmental services for America's low-income, pre-school children aged three to five, and social services for their families. Approximately 1 400 community-based non-profit organisations and school systems develop programmes to meet the needs of this target group.

three years. For children over three, governments generally provide free pre-school education, most often through direct provision in public institutions. In the Nordic countries, although services for the over-threes are generally not free until the pre-school year, costs are affordable and are based on means testing, with low-income groups paying low or token fees. For children under three years, costs for services are generally shared between parents and public authorities (in the Netherlands, with employers also). Public authorities subsidise services through direct local authority provision (Denmark, Finland, Sweden), or through direct funding to providers, including private providers (Netherlands, Norway) or through indirect subsidies, such as family cash benefits (Australia, United States), tax credits (Belgium, United Kingdom) and employer contributions (Belgium, Italy, Netherlands). In only three of the twelve countries reviewed (Denmark, Finland, Sweden) is the public provision of high-quality ECEC for children from their first year considered an entitlement, on an equal footing with services for older children.

For under-three services, parents contribute on average 25-30% of the costs, varying from a 15% parental contribution in Finland to over 70% of service costs borne by parents in the United States. Research of 100 counties in the United States suggests that the parental fee level determines the levels of both demand and supply of ECEC services (Edwards *et al.*, 1996). The researchers suggest that to raise the utilisation of early childhood services by low-income groups, the following strategies should be applied in combination: a) lower the costs for parents by indirect parental subsidies, *e.g.* tax reductions, childcare vouchers or benefits, and reductions for siblings; and b) increase the perceived quality of early childhood services by staffing requirements and accreditation regulations. Many European countries with long-established regulatory and accreditation systems in place apply these strategies consistently, and may in addition, directly subsidise public services so that overall costs to parents are low. Moderate costs are charged for infants and toddlers in public services, but free access is provided by entitlement for all children: from two-and-a-half years in Belgium; from three years in Italy; and from four years in the Netherlands, Sweden and the United

Kingdom. The Nordic countries generally retain some parental charges up to the year before entry into compulsory schooling, but these are related to family income and are generally waived completely for low-income families.

4.2 Are children at risk sufficiently provided for?

As insufficient public investment generally falls disproportionately on disadvantaged neighbourhoods, affordability for low-income families remains a problem in all but a few countries. In the United States, for example, only 45% of 3- to 5-year-olds from low-income families were enrolled in pre-school programmes, compared with almost 75% from high-income families (National Education Goals Panel, 1997). The situation is currently improving, with more generous subsidies being made available to low- and middle-income families, but according to American specialists, the situation is urgent in the major cities: 45% of children entering kindergarten in the United States are from at-risk backgrounds, while the figure reaches 65% of all children in the large cities (Zill and West, 2000). Even when cash benefits and tax credits to cover childcare expenses are provided, appropriate provision for families and children at risk seems difficult to ensure.[5] As these families are often those who would benefit most from quality ECEC, there is a need to target funds effectively to them.

4.3 Can resources be better spent?

Even where public funding increases, new challenges appear, including: effectively managing welfare pluralism where the state complements the resources found in the voluntary and for-profit sectors; developing performance assessment tools to ensure value for money; and redistributing costs across the education system in a more equitable manner. There are good reasons to shift resources to younger children, especially towards the socially disadvantaged, as there are high social returns for investments in this group (OECD, 1999).

---

5. Evidence from Australia, the United Kingdom and the United States suggests that support to ECEC provision through demand subsidies may lead to shortages in low-income areas where both for-profit and non-profit operators find it difficult to survive.

Evidence of these developments could be seen in the countries reviewed by the OECD, where policy makers were engaged in:

– Expanding services while maintaining cost increases at a reasonable level;

– Improved monitoring of the levels and uses of public funding;

– Improved regulation and tighter agreements between central and local authorities, with support to these authorities to undertake cost-benefit and needs assessment analyses;

– Re-grouping small authorities to obtain more effective management of services;

– Reducing excessive demand through better assessment of family needs, and monitoring of parental leave; and

– Making use of public-private partnerships, through competition and other mechanisms, to bring down the cost of services (*e.g.* user charges for those who can afford to pay, use of tendering, and contracting out).

5. PARTICIPATORY APPROACHES TO QUALITY IMPROVEMENT

The benefits of early childhood education and care rely crucially on good-quality provision. Pressures for quality improvement and assessment are increasing as parents become better informed and governments take responsibility for services. However, many countries have inherited unhelpful burdens from the past:

– *Unregulated provision for infants linked to traditional understandings of the role of the state vis-à-vis families and young children.* In some countries, a majority of young children under three remain for at least part of the working day in the care of unregistered child-minders and/or providers.

– *Excessive focus on care and protection.* Many countries need to move towards a more developmental approach and to ensure that centres become stimulating places for young children (NICHD, 2000). Such a move is needed, particularly in traditional "care" services and in all programmes for children at risk of educational failure.

– *Employment of poorly trained, under-paid staff.* The predominant care-and-protection attitudes of

the past have meant that services for infants and toddlers were seen as relatively undemanding, and were often staffed by untrained personnel. The situation is reinforced in countries where private provision remains unregulated, or is not sufficiently subsidised to make it economically viable to employ well-trained personnel.

– *Placing of young children in formal learning situations from the age of three or four years.* During the 1970s and 1980s, many governments invested heavily in providing free, universal coverage to all children from the age of three, four or five years. In doing so, they tended to reproduce the learning environments, child-staff ratios, teaching approaches and assessment procedures of formal schooling, which are often inappropriate for the age group and the social profile of the children targeted by public early childhood services.

5.1 Government leadership

Faced with these challenges, OECD countries have invested in different strategies to improve quality. These include a commitment to better resourcing and regulation, including improved child-staff ratios, formal regulation of staff recruitment and qualifications, and supplementary investments to improve services for children at risk. The experience of the OECD review suggests that central and local governments have a pivotal role in these areas. Among the many challenges they face are:

– To formulate clear national goals for early childhood services;

– To establish financing and management structures that enable these goals to be achieved;

– To ensure that buildings, staff, pedagogical and support services are available;

– To ensure equitable access and high quality services for young children at risk of educational failure;

– To ensure quality, accredit services and regulate staff qualifications, group sizes and child-staff ratios; and

– To establish supportive monitoring and evaluation systems.

In recent years, OECD governments have made much progress in providing such leadership. A far more energetic and professional management of early childhood services is now evident in almost all countries. OECD review teams noted, for example:

– The use of regulation and fiscal measures to discourage unlicensed provision. In Belgium, for example, parents can only benefit from tax relief when they use day centres – public or private – registered and supervised by public authorities;

– Consultation with regional and local government, social partners, professional organisations, and parent groups to formulate clear policies, eliminate waste and improve quality in the system;

– Provision of special funding and support to build up technical management competencies at local levels, *e.g.* in the Netherlands and Sweden;

– The formulation of framework documents that guide programmatic and curricular activities across the system, *e.g.* Norway and Belgium; and

– Support for the creation of voluntary standards, codes of ethics, guidelines and recommendations, *e.g.* in Australia, the Netherlands, and the United States.

5.2 The need for pedagogical frameworks based on consultation

An important means to assure quality is the formulation of national pedagogical frameworks for the early years, with intensive in-service training of teachers to understand and follow their basic principles. In several countries, *e.g.* Finland, such guidelines have been formulated after a wide process of consultation, giving ownership to a broad range of stakeholders. In addition, in the Nordic countries, staff and parents have the further responsibility of establishing the centre's more detailed curriculum and pedagogical plan, based on the national pedagogical framework and the local municipality's objectives.

National pedagogical frameworks identify the key goals of early childhood services, inform parents and practitioners how young children develop and learn, and outline how early childhood centres should support children's learning (*e.g.* Norwegian Ministry of Children and Family Affairs, 1996; New Zealand Ministry of Education, 1996). They may

also cover the social and civic attitudes that a country may wish to see inform early education (Swedish Ministry of Education and Science, 1998), or identify important learning areas or emphasise the physical, relational and programmatic requirements of quality learning environments (Bredekamp and Copple, 1997; Harms *et al.*, 1998; Italian Ministry of Education, 1991). Without such guidelines, inexperienced or untrained staff may easily revert to direct instruction as their default mode or – presuming that children learn intuitively when placed with other children in enriched learning environments – adopt a *laissez-faire* approach to programmes and the acquisition of basic skills.

Leaving aside the particular learning areas that countries propose in their frameworks – whether national culture, visual arts, early literacy, social skills or civic values – what are the core programme features that pedagogical frameworks should emphasise? Given the importance of cultural preferences, and the wide variation of the needs of children within and across countries, the question is perhaps impossible to answer. If we assume, however, that all early childhood centres should deliver at least the basic goals designed for children in need of special educational support, then national pedagogical frameworks would direct centres: to ensure the health and motor development of each child; to nurture self-regulation, language and socio-relational skills; to develop communication and reasoning skills; and to provide an adequate response to each child's learning characteristics and needs. Bowman *et al.* (2000) also recommend as a requirement for effective pre-school programmes outreach to parents and their involvement. While some research suggests that parental involvement brings a weak or only a temporary contribution to cognitive gains obtained from educational programmes (White *et al.*, 1992), intuitively, the recommendation seems well-founded. Family support programmes and networking with professional ECEC and school staff probably do help in sustaining the developmental and educational gains of a quality early childhood programme, and in lessening the effects of adverse child-rearing conditions in at-risk families (Harbin *et al.*, 2000). Likewise, research from Britain suggests that cognitive and language gains are strongly supported by parental involvement in children's literacy at home (Siraj-Blatchford, 2000; Sylva, 2000).

5.3 Wider participation in defining and ensuring quality

A notable contribution to improving quality is ownership by staff of the programme and their continued efforts to improve it as a team. In several countries, these efforts are now made possible by the support of inspection and advisory bodies for structured self-evaluation programmes. In England, for example, the Effective Early Learning (EEL) instrument, developed by University College Worcester, is widely used to guide early childhood centres undertaking a systematic process of self-evaluation that is supported and validated externally by trained professionals (Bertram and Pascal, 1997). The EEL encourages discussion and reflection by staff on their programme, their attitudes and practice towards children and parents, as well as on the more technical aspects of administration, finance and planning. Thanks to the process, which normally takes place over several months, centres define their own programmes and approaches, appropriate to their community circumstances.

Participatory approaches are especially useful in improving process, *i.e.* what is actually occurring in programmes. For example, the Early Childhood Environment Rating Scale (ECERS) – devised by Harms *et al.* (1998) in the United States – examines personal care routines, furnishings, language, reasoning experiences, motor activities, creative activities, social development and staff needs. Process quality analysis may also focus on interactions among staff, among children, and between children and staff, as well as on partnerships with parents, and the learning and social opportunities offered. Participatory instruments can provide a sense of ownership and control for staff as they strive to improve their practice. They are a means not only of finding out how children are developing but also of supporting the practice of educators, leading them to constructive self-assessment and change in order to become "reflective practitioners" (Moss and Pence, 1994).

6. APPROPRIATE TRAINING AND WORK CONDITIONS FOR ALL STAFF

Staff working with children in ECEC programmes have a major impact on children's early development and learning. Research shows that training, status, pay and working conditions are important determinants of recruitment and retention, and are strong predictors of programme quality (CQCO, 1995; European Commission Childcare Network, 1996*a*). In particular, staff who have more formal education and more specialised early childhood training provide more stimulating, warm, and supportive interactions with children (Phillipsen *et al.*, 1997).

The way in which staff are recruited and trained depends to a large extent on the degree to which the ECEC sector develops its own identity relative to other parts of the education system, and also on the relationship between the caring and educating roles within the sector. In the Nordic countries, early childhood provision is viewed as a unified socio-educational service for children from 0-6 years and as a social support system for their families. This creates a unified profession for those working with children across the age-range, who are trained at tertiary level, and are considered to have a different, but equally important, role to school teachers. Elsewhere, however, the dichotomy between education and care has persisted. Within the education sector, pre-school teachers are trained at tertiary level, but not always with sufficient specialisation in working with young children and their families. Early childhood specialists are concerned that when early year teachers and primary teachers are trained together, as in Australia, the Netherlands, the United Kingdom and the United States, the greater weight of primary teaching seems to influence training more than the specific skills and approaches of early childhood pedagogy. The UK is introducing new standards in 2002 to bring early childhood training more into line with the specific nature of the field.

6.1 The recruitment challenge: volume and diversity

Many countries are experiencing growing recruitment and retention difficulties, particularly in the traditional "care" sector, outside the education field. It is not clear whether the challenge is temporary or long-term, but the issue has become acute in some countries. In Australia, the Netherlands, and the United States, annual staff turnover may reach over 30% in centre-based ECEC. Two key challenges are:

— *To maintain a sufficient volume of recruitment to meet the future needs of the sector.* This will not be easy: it is proving increasingly hard to recruit young people, especially into the childcare sector. Reasons include low status, low salaries and strenuous working conditions, high child-staff ratios, long hours, little or no paid leave, limited access to in-service training, and limited career mobility (Penn, 2000). In addition, the growing diversification of providers, including a high proportion of family day-care settings and private providers, brings greater variation in employment contracts, working conditions, and career prospects within the sector (Christopherson, 1997).

— *To recruit employees whose profiles match the growing diversity of children.* According to centre directors and managers in inner-city neighbourhoods, personnel from diverse ethnic and cultural backgrounds need to be much more present in services that cater for children from such backgrounds – both in terms of equal opportunity and also for the efficacy of these services, one of whose aims is to promote social cohesion. In this respect, social welfare services seem to be more successful than the traditional education services, but with the dilemma that in general, personnel are not as well-trained as in education.

6.2 Concerns about the present training of ECEC staff

There is general consensus that investment in raising training levels is one key to solving recruitment difficulties. Levels of training are rising in all countries, with a minimum three-year tertiary-level diploma or university degree for teachers, and a minimum three-year, post-16 vocational diploma for childcare workers becoming the norm. In both cases, intensive practical training is also generally required, including placements in settings addressing special needs. Yet, concerns are still evident.

Teacher training remains too abstract. This concern arises particularly in countries where training has only recently shifted to the university sector (*e.g.* Finland, Italy, Portugal), although the successful integration of teacher training colleges into the university system in the Scandinavian countries shows that appropriate training at the university level is possible, which includes important modules on child development, care, pedagogy and outreach to parents.

Training does not respond quickly enough to current needs. For example, the new emphasis on working with parents and family members is not always well covered in training. There is also a lack of specialised training for those who work with infants and toddlers, even though provision for this age group is expanding in many countries. Nor is the growing requirement to work with multi-cultural communities and with students with various special needs always reflected in training programmes.

There is insufficient attention to recruitment and initial training of family day-care providers. In many countries, levels of education and training of family day-care providers are well below those found among centre- and school-based staff. A majority of providers have no prior training to work with young children, and may even be exempt from any training and educational requirements. There is a growing need to upgrade the sector and create incentives for workers to enter the field. A number of countries already encourage family day-carers to be employed within organised, publicly funded networks; or require them to complete a pre-service vocational qualification.

6.3 Creating a flexible, modular career

In systems split between "care" and "education", the training routes in each domain offer different areas of expertise, and are fairly inflexible across this divide. Traditionally, there has been little career opportunity for lower-skilled workers, including family day-carers, to move from one area to another, and in particular, to qualify for more skilled and better paid positions. Countries have been adopting various routes to greater flexibility. In Denmark, for example, relatively mature students are being recruited with weight given to their prior work experience. Sweden enables trained childcare assistants to progress to university training for pre-school teachers, and also gives credit for prior experience. Such strategies are particularly important for countries that have recently increased qualifications (*e.g.* Italy, Portugal) and are seeking to reconcile tensions between university-educated entrants and those in the field with little training.

Flexibility can also be interpreted to mean employing lower-skilled staff at lower wages, alongside a smaller number of well-trained staff. This can provide benefits in terms of expanding provision within manageable costs, but can also cause tensions, and raises the wider issue about the priority given to early childhood development. At present only Denmark, Finland and Sweden commit high levels of public funding across the entire early childhood period.

6.4 Expanding in-service training and professional development

In-service training and professional development are crucial to improving ECEC, yet opportunities are uneven. Staff with the lowest levels of initial training tend to have the least access, and family day-care providers and small centres in rural areas have difficulty participating, especially where there is only one staff member for each group of children. Quality of training varies, and human resource expertise can be limited.

A key priority is to create opportunities for planning and self-evaluation among staff to produce a co-operative working environment. In Belgium, Italy, Norway and Portugal, non-contact time is set aside for staff development as an essential part of forging staff relationships and of undertaking an ongoing critical evaluation of the programme being offered to children (European Commission Childcare Network, 1996b). In Italy, six hours a week are set aside as non-contact time to allow staff to undertake, for example, pedagogical documentation, a very useful tool in deepening understanding and encouraging reflection.

6.5 Recruiting a more diverse workforce

Several promising approaches to facilitate the entry of workers reflecting the origins of children found in early childhood services are being tried. Efforts are made especially in the traditional child-care field where the engagement of local staff is more widespread than in pre-schools. For example, a tenet of the Head Start programme in the United States is to employ parents and volunteers from the local community. Many complete the Child Development Associate Qualification and continue to work in centres after their children have "graduated". Several countries recruit staff of immigrant backgrounds – some of whom were trained teachers in their home countries – to work as bilingual ECEC assistants. In the Netherlands and Belgium, ethnic minority parents have been employed to provide a bridge to the local community.

7. ATTENTION TO EVALUATION, MONITORING AND DATA COLLECTION

Governments today are aware that quality early childhood services make a solid contribution to education, social and economic policies. With few exceptions, the debate about services for young children shifted in the OECD countries during the 1990s from whether governments should invest in early childhood services to how provision should be effectively financed, organised and managed (OECD, 2001a), and how quality might be ensured. By its nature, however, the ECEC field is a complex one. Due to the variety of agencies involved, the diversity of services both formal and informal, and weaknesses in both data collection and policy co-ordination, it can be difficult to form a clear picture of the provision and its effectiveness.

7.1 Evaluation studies

With the growing professionalisation of the early childhood field, and more widespread recognition of the value of early childhood programmes to young children, greater attention is being paid to the evaluation of programmes. The United States is probably the leader in this field, not only because of its research capability, but also because many of its programmes are funded by agencies that demand proof from providers that programmes are functioning correctly, and that children are actually reaching agreed objectives. More accountability can also be seen today in publicly funded programmes in other countries, e.g. in 2000, the Netherlands completed a large-scale evaluation of two experimental pre-school programmes Kaleidoscoop (Dutch High/Scope) and Piramide, comparing them with regular pre-school and kindergarten education (Veen et al., 2000). Similarly, the UK government is engaged in a comprehensive review of the Early Excellence Centres programme.

It would seem useful to extend such research-led evaluations to system-wide national programmes. For example, a recent cross-national study found consistently across five European countries that centres in education-oriented systems were marked by lower structural and process quality than centres in more developmentally-oriented ones (Cryer *et al.*, 1999). Such a study deserves further investigation and extension by independent research bodies, with the aim of improving the quality of programmes in national pre-school systems.

7.2 Expanding and improving data collections

A useful first step would be the *redefinition and expansion of data collections*, to include all publicly funded early education and care services for young children. This would encompass not only pre-primary education for the 3-6 year-olds but also other registered provision such as, family day-care, day-care centres, after-school care, and special services.

Second, it would be helpful for policy makers to have reliable figures on *public and private subsidies targeted to young children, disaggregated to cover key elements of expenditure* (expenditure on the various ECEC service types; expenditure on maternity and parental leave; expenditure on child allowances and other transfers to families with young children, including public cash benefits, tax credits and employer contributions to cover childcare expenses).[6] Financial tracking helps to inform planning and resource allocation, and contributes to accountability.

Third, systems would gain greatly from *the development of specific indicators for the early childhood field*. This would not only allow child outcomes to be appropriately identified and assessed, but would also provide an idea of the impact of contextual and process factors on young children.

Fourth, *more dynamic methods of statistical analysis* are required that enable treatment of data from the different domains of early childhood systems as interactive variables, whose impact on system goals can be measured with some degree of accuracy.

Fifth, *a focus on the key issues of demand, supply, equitable access and quality* is required (Olmsted, 2001). As these issues have yet to be satisfactorily resolved

for early childhood services in most countries, particularly for the 0-3 year age-group, the indicators chosen should be capable of providing adequate information to forecast and plan provision, and to measure the quality and appropriateness of services offered to different groups of children.

7.3 Developing indicators to monitor child outcomes

It can be seen from the OECD comparative review that different countries choose or stress different child outcomes, influenced by their views of childhood, the history of their early childhood systems, or by the particular needs of their child populations at a given moment (OECD, 2001*a*). In the English-speaking countries, with many at-risk children in their societies, ministries or large-scale agencies are concerned to obtain a measure of the learning achievement of young children, or at least, of their "readiness for school".[7] Different types of assessment are used: child testing by professionals using standardised test items; ongoing assessments by either test professionals or teaching staff; and teacher-administered exit or entry tests.[8]

In other countries, with more child-centred, developmentally-oriented systems, there is little demand that young children should be assessed, even through "light" sample surveys. In these countries, there is a reluctance to place pressure on young children. There may exist also a strong

---

6. In Norway, the Ministry of Children and Family Affairs compiles the annual expenditure on children across all ministries into one document to show what is spent on children, as well as to formulate objectives and policy for children across sectors.

7. Several critiques of the concept of "school readiness" have been formulated, but it also can be appreciated that governments and funders are required to provide evidence about what young children actually learn in early childhood centres.

8. Bowman *et al.* (2000) explain that although there is overlap in the use of the words "test" and "assessment", the former refers to a standardised instrument, formally administered and designed to minimize all differences in the conditions of testing. Assessments tend on the contrary to use multiple instruments (*e.g.* observations, performance measures, interviews, portfolios and examples of children's work) and take place over a longer period of time.

distrust of early literacy assessment, which is seen as: a) engendering a potentially negative focus on the child; b) distracting attention from structural, process and programmatic requirements of quality approaches; and c) deflecting teacher attention from wider developmental goals. In sum, the development of indicators across the OECD countries against which children's learning and development could be measured prior to primary schooling, needs a strong rationale before it will gain the support of a broad range of countries.

If it is agreed that some form of central monitoring and assessment of child outcomes is helpful and needed, then further challenges face early childhood authorities. Firstly, what form should assessment take; secondly, what should be the central content areas for assessment; and thirdly, what measures would provide a useful indication of development and learning achieved by children at this age?

At the moment, agreement on the first two questions seems easier to reach than a clear reply to the third. In line with practice across most countries, the National Council on Measurement in Education in the United States recommends that assessment be grounded in *multiple* sources of information, including interviews, observations, work sampling and informal teacher and peer assessments over a period of time (NCME, 1999). Many of these assessment procedures are already in place in the more developmental early childhood systems.

Where the content areas for assessment are concerned, research in the United States points to the need to include developmental as well as cognitive indicators, in keeping with the holistic goals of early childhood systems. As noted earlier, the National Education Goals Panel (1997) recommends that as children mature, attention to the following dimensions can contribute significantly to the child's well-being and success in school: health and physical development; emotional well-being and social competence; positive approaches to learning; communication skills; appropriate general knowledge; and cognitive skills. There is also growing agreement in the United States and other countries, that quality goals for children should be specified at multiple levels – parental

and local as well as national – and with increasing customisation and specificity (Kagan and Cohen, 1997).

Further challenges for countries will be to screen children effectively (taking account of socio-economic background, at-risk factors, presence of learning difficulties and so on), and to link child-related variables with structural factors that have an important impact on outcomes, *e.g.* policy frameworks, level of funding, affordability; regulatory and monitoring frameworks, staff profiles, and with key characteristics of the learning environment. If these factors can be reliably linked with measures of developmental and learning outcomes, the process may yield – as in the recent PISA assessment of 15-year-olds (OECD, 2001*b*) – valuable information for policy development and programme improvement.

8. A FRAMEWORK AND LONG-TERM AGENDA FOR RESEARCH AND EVALUATION

With the rapid pace of change in early childhood education, it becomes necessary for countries to keep national research and evaluation up to date. This requires a planned research agenda backed by long-term funding. The following types of research can strengthen the knowledge base – although the balance of research requirements will vary by country.

Socio-cultural studies analyse early childhood and child rearing and seek to challenge taken-for-granted approaches to child policies and practice (Dahlberg *et al.*, 1999). These studies are enriched by perspectives from other disciplines, such as economics, history, anthropology, sociology, gender studies, and public policy. Important questions to investigate include: How is childhood changing? How is this change linked to new awareness of gender equity? How does a particular nation or culture view the issue of child rearing? How does childhood differ from one milieu to another within the same society? What are the purposes of early childhood institutions? How are quality criteria and outcome goals arrived at? How do societies understand knowledge, learning, care?

Comparative, cross-national research can identify specific policies and practices from which people in other countries can draw inspiration. Their main value is not to identify "models" for imitation or to construct league tables, but to assist policy makers in thinking more broadly about ECEC. Comparative research links with both policy research and socio-cultural theory, and provides a prism or lens to assess the unquestioned assumptions, discourses and practices of one's own country (Moss, 2001). For example, given the very wide range of child-staff ratios practised across different countries, it would be useful for policy makers to have reliable research on the ratios to adopt with different age-groups, in terms of cost, efficacy and cultural expectations (see Tobin, 1999).

Longitudinal studies and large-scale surveys have been initiated in several countries, but are particularly used in the United States. They help to clarify the relationships between young children's experiences inside and outside the home and subsequent outcomes in childhood and beyond. Comprehensive data collected on a representative sample at different intervals allow researchers to study – in depth and over time – many of the important issues for children in contemporary society, including whether exposure to different early childhood programmes is associated with different outcomes.

Country-specific policy research examines, for example, broad policy issues and choices faced by countries, often with regard to the relationship between cost and outcomes, as illustrated for example by the ongoing Cost, Quality and Children Outcomes studies initiated in the United States from 1993 (CQCO, 1995). It may include also evaluations of large-scale public programmes or of specific programme types, for example to show the effects of different programmes on the learning outcomes of specific groups of children (see Barnett, 1995; OECD, 1999). A strong example of this type of research is again provided by the United States, where the US Department of Education and the US Department Health and Human Resources are supported by the various official or officially funded national research agencies in early childhood and education, *e.g.* the National Center for Education Statistics, and the National Institute on Early Childhood Development and Education. Private foundations and independent professional bodies are also important in the American system

in researching and orienting early childhood policy, *e.g.* the Packard Foundation, and the National Association for the Education of Young Children. In contrast, the volume of government-sponsored research on national early childhood issues coming from other countries with long-established early childhood systems seems rather less, although it may be possible that research from European countries is not being accessed internationally because of language (see Boocock, 1995).

Over the past decades, *psychological research on young children and their learning* has developed greatly, moving from a behavioural genetics perspective in the 1960s and 1970s, to a more developmental and interactionist paradigm. In line with Brofenbrenner's (1986) critique of behavioural genetics, recent neuro-science research shows that complex skill development is essentially "experience dependent" and requires structured experience through social interaction, that is, modelling, guidance and support from the outside by parents and other care-givers (Leseman, 2002). In unfavourable environments, *e.g.* in dysfunctional families and neighbourhoods where at-risk factors accumulate, the actualisation of the genetic potential of the child is threatened and obstacles to optimal development are created, leading frequently to the under-development of language and socio-cognitive skills. New insights into brain and cognitive development and better understanding of physical and socio-emotional development are helping to inform not only classroom practice, but also the attitudes of policy makers and funding agencies.

Research on practice and process undertaken by local centres and staff can be extremely valuable both in enabling staff to reflect on their own practice, and in providing information to policy makers. Some countries, such as Sweden, have integrated research methodology and practice into the pre-training of ECEC professionals. In other countries, reflection on practice is encouraged through government-funded renewal programmes, through the practice of documentation (*e.g.* Reggio Emilia in Italy) or through participatory self-evaluation instruments (*e.g.* the United Kingdom). In yet others, staff research is led by local university early childhood departments (*e.g.* Finland); pedagogical advisors (*e.g.* Denmark); or by various model programmes that encourage ongoing research and team training.

CONCLUSION

There has been tremendous development of early childhood policy making across OECD countries in recent years. This chapter has described how those responsible for this area of policy are increasingly developing a vision for the whole sector. The chapter also reviewed the steps needed to sustain progress. Many areas require attention: resource mobilisation; goal-setting and standard-setting; planning and mapping of services; partnership development; recruitment, training and staff support; quality improvement; the monitoring of system quality and the learning achievement of children; and research, indicator development and data collection. Rising expectations for early childhood services can only increase the magnitude of these important tasks.

In confronting these challenges, policy makers will take into account a growing concern in our societies for individual rights and equity, a concern that underlines state responsibility to ensure the well-being of children and to guarantee a fair start in life for all. In this context, the triangular relationship between children, parents and the state is changing rapidly. As citizens, young children are seen to have a right both to the protection of the state, and to public support for early childhood services where they can thrive, feel involved and learn in ways appropriate to their age and needs. No doubt, this new emphasis on the place of children in our society will influence early childhood policy making in future years, and improve the quality of services organised for our young citizens.

References

BARNETT, W. (1995), "Long-term effects of early childhood programs on cognitive and school outcomes", *The Future of Children: Long-term Outcomes of Early Childhood Programs*, Vol. 5, No. 3.

BERTRAM, A. and **PASCAL, C.** (1997), "A conceptual framework for evaluating effectiveness in early childhood settings", in M. Karlsson Lohmander (ed.), *Research in Early Childhood: Settings in Interaction*, Gothenburg University, Gothenburg.

BOOCOCK, S. (1995), "Early childhood programs in other nations: goals and outcomes", in R. Behrman (ed.), *The Future of Children*, Packard Foundation, Los Altos, CA.

BOWMAN, B., DONOVAN, M. and **BURNS, M.** (eds.) (2000), *Eager to Learn: Educating our Preschoolers*, National Academy Press, Washington, DC.

BREDEKAMP, S. and **COPPLE, C.** (eds.) (1997), *Developmentally Appropriate Practice in Early Childhood Programs*, National Association for the Education of Young Children, Washington, DC.

BROFENBRENNER, U. (1986), *Reality and Research in the Ecology of Human Development*, American Psychological Association.

CHRISTOPHERSON, S. (1997), "Childcare and elderly care: what occupational opportunities for women?", Labour Market and Social Policy Occasional Papers No. 27, OECD, Paris.

CQCO – Cost, Quality, and Outcomes Study Team (1995), *Cost, Quality and Child Outcomes in Child Care Centers*, University of Colorado at Denver, Colorado.

CRYER, D., TIETZE, W., BURCHINAL, M., LEAL, T. and **PALACIOS, J.** (1999), "Predicting process quality from structural quality in preschool programs: A cross-country comparison", *Early Childhood Research Quarterly*, Vol. 14(3), pp. 339-361.

DAHLBERG, G., MOSS, P. and **PENCE, A.** (eds.) (1999), *Beyond Quality in Early Childhood Education and Care: Postmodern Perspectives*, Taylor and Francis, London.

DENTON, K. and **WEST, J.** (2002), *Children's Reading and Mathematics Achievement in Kindergarten and First Grade*, NCES, Washington, DC.

DOCKETT, S. and **PERRY, B.** (2001), "Starting school: effective transitions", *Early Childhood Research and Practice*, Vol. 3, No. 2.

EDWARDS, J., FULLER, B. and **LIANG, X.** (1996), "The mixed preschool market: explaining local variation in family demand and organized supply", *Economics of Education Review*, Vol. 15, No. 2, pp. 149-161.

ESO (1999), *Daycare and Incentives – A Summary*, Swedish Finance Department, Stockholm.

EUROPEAN COMMISSION CHILDCARE NETWORK (1996a), *Quality Targets in Services for Young Children*, Brussels.

EUROPEAN COMMISSION CHILDCARE NETWORK (1996b), A *Review of Services for Young Children in the European Union 1990-1995*, Brussels.

EUROSTAT (2000), *Key Data on Education in Europe*, 1999-2000, European Commission, Luxembourg.

FRASER, H. (2002), "Early intervention in literacy and numeracy", The Scottish Executive, Early Years Matters, Edinburgh.

GARDNER, H. (2000), *Intelligence Reframed: Multiple Intelligences for the 21st Century*, Basic Books, New York.

HARBIN, G., MCWILLIAM, R. and **GALLAGHER, J.** (2000), "Services for young children with disabilities and their families", in J. Shonkoff and S. Meisels (eds), *Handbook of Early Childhood Intervention*, Cambridge University Press, Cambridge.

HARMS, T., CRYER D. and **CLIFFORD, R.** (1998), *Early Childhood Environment Rating Scale*, Teachers College Press, New York.

ITALIAN MINISTRY OF EDUCATION (1991), *Scuola Materna : Orientamenti educativi e didattici*, Rome.

KAGAN, S. and **COHEN. N.** (1997), *Solving the Quality Crisis: A Vision for America's Child Care System*, Yale University Bush Center, New Haven.

KEMPSON, E. (1996), *Life on a Low Income*, Joseph Rowntree Foundation, York.

KUCERA, K. and **BAUER, T.** (2001), *Does Childcare Pay Off? Evidence for Costs and Benefits of Daycare Centres in Zurich*, Department of Social Services, Zurich.

LESEMAN, P. (2002), *Early Childhood Education and Care for Children from Low-income or Minority Backgrounds*, OECD, Paris (in press).

LESEMAN, P., OTTER, M.E., BLOK H. and **DECKERS, P.** (1998), "Effects of pre- and early education centre-based programmes. A meta-analysis of studies published from 1985 to 1996", *Netherlands tijdschrift voor opdoeving en onderwijs*, Vol. 14, No. 3, pp. 134-154.

MORRIS, P. *et al.* (2001), *How Welfare and Work Policies Affect Children: A Synthesis of Research*, Manpower Demonstration Research Corp., New York.

MOSS, P. (2001), "Workforce issues in early childhood education and care", in S. Kamerman (ed), *Early Childhood Education and Care: International Perspectives*, Institute for Child and Family Policy, Columbia University, New York.

MOSS, P. and **PENCE, A.** (eds.) (1994), *Valuing Quality in Early Childhood Services: New Approaches to Defining Quality*, Paul Chapman, London.

NATIONAL CENTER FOR EARLY DEVELOPMENT AND LEARNING (2000), *Enhancing the Transition to Kindergarten*, University of Virginia, VA.

NATIONAL EDUCATION GOALS PANEL (1997), *Special Early Childhood Report*, Washington D.C.

NCME (1999), *Standards for Educational and Psychological Testing*, AERA Publications, Washington D.C.

NEW ZEALAND MINISTRY OF EDUCATION (1996), *Te Whariki Early Childhood Curriculum*, Wellington.

NICHD EARLY CHILD CARE RESEARCH NETWORK (2000), "The relation of child care to cognitive and language development", *Child Development*, Vol. 71, pp. 960-980.

NORWEGIAN MINISTRY OF CHILDREN AND FAMILY AFFAIRS (1996), *Framework Plan for Daycare Institutions*, Oslo.

OBSERVATOIRE DE L'ENFANCE (2001), *État des lieux de l'accueil des enfants de 2,5 à 12 ans en dehors des heures scolaires*, Brussels.

OECD (1999), "Early childhood education and care: getting the most from the investment", *Education Policy Analysis*, Paris.

OECD (2001a), *Starting Strong: Early Childhood Education and Care*, Paris.

OECD (2001*b*), *Knowledge and Skills for Life: First Results from* PISA 2000, Paris.

OECD (2002), *Education at a Glance:* OECD Indicators 2002, Paris.

OLMSTED, P. (2001), *Data Collection and System Monitoring*, UNESCO, Paris.

PENN, H. (ed.) (2000), *Early Childhood Services: Theory, Policy and Practice*, Open University, Buckingham.

PHILLIPSEN, L., BURCHINAL, M., HOWES, C. and **CRYER, D.** (1997), "The prediction of process quality from structural features of child care", *Early Childhood Research Quarterly*, Vol. 12, pp. 281-303.

SAMEROFF, A. and **FIESE, B.** (2000), "Early childhood intervention: a continuing evolution", in J. Shonkoff and S. Meisels (eds.), *Handbook of Early Childhood Intervention*, Cambridge University Press, Cambridge.

SCHULMAN, K., BLANK, H. and **EWEN, D.** (1999), *Seeds of Success*, State Prekindergarten Initiatives 1998-1999, Children's Defense Fund, Washington, DC.

SHONKOFF, J. and **PHILLIPS, D.** (eds.) (2000), *From Neurons to Neighborhoods: The Science of Early Childhood Development*, National Academy Press, Washington, DC.

SHORE, R. (1997), *Re-thinking the Brain: New Insights into Early Development*, Families and Work Institute, New York.

SIRAJ-BLATCHFORD, I. (ed.) (2000), *Supporting Identity, Diversity and Language in the Early Years*, Open University Press, Buckingham.

SWEDISH MINISTRY OF EDUCATION AND SCIENCE (1998), *Curriculum for Pre-School*, Stockholm.

SYLVA, K. (2000), *Effective Provision of Pre-school Education* (EPPE Research Project), Oxford.

TOBIN, J. (1999), "Using cross-cultural research to question taken-for-granted beliefs in American early childhood education", in G. Brougère and S. Rayna (eds.), *Culture, Enfance et Éducation Préscolaire*, UNESCO, Paris.

URRUTIA, M. (1999), *The Impact of Early Childhood Intervention Programs on Economic Growth and Equity*, Inter-American Development Bank, Washington DC.

VAN DER GAAG, J. (2002), *From Child Development to Human Development*, University of Amsterdam, Faculty of Economics and Econometrics, Amsterdam.

VANDELL, D. and **WOLFE, B.** (2000), *Child Care Quality: Does it Matter and Does it Need to be Improved?*, US Department of Health and Human Services, Washington, DC.

VEEN, A., ROELEVELD, J. and **LESEMAN, P.** (2000), *Evaluatie van Kaleidoscoop en Piramide*, Eindrapportage, SCO Kohnstamm Instituut [Evaluation of Kaleidoscoop and Piramide. Final report], Amsterdam.

VERRY, D. (2000), "Some economic aspects of early childhood education and care", *International Journal of Educational Research*, Vol. 33, No. 1, pp. 95-122.

WHITE, K., TAYLOR, M. and **MOSS, V.** (1992), "Does research support claims about the benefits of involving parents in early intervention programs?", *Review of Educational Research*, Vol. 62.

ZILL, N. and **WEST, J.** (2000), *Entering Kindergarten: A Portrait of American Children When They Begin School*, NCES, Washington, DC.

Data for Figure 1.1

Net enrolment rates by single year of age in pre-primary[1] and primary education, 2000 (%)

	Pre-primary education				Primary education			
	3-year-olds	4-year-olds	5-year-olds	6-year-olds	3-year-olds	4-year-olds	5-year-olds	6-year-olds
Australia	16.4	50.1	32.5	0.0	0.0	1.6	68.7	100.5
Austria	39.3	79.6	89.4	32.7	0.0	0.0	0.0	62.5
Belgium	98.2	99.2	97.8	4.8	0.0	0.0	1.2	94.7
Canada	0.0	39.9	88.4	0.0	0.0	0.0	0.0	101.9
Czech Republic	54.9	81.0	98.0	47.2	0.0	0.0	0.1	52.8
Denmark	71.8	90.6	96.6	95.6	0.0	0.0	0.0	4.4
Finland	33.9	41.9	49.6	72.7	0.0	0.0	0.0	1.0
France	100.7	101.9	100.0	1.4	0.0	0.0	1.4	100.3
Germany	54.8	81.4	83.8	65.0	0.0	0.0	0.0	48.9
Greece	0.0	57.6	87.1	0.0	0.0	0.0	2.9	99.5
Hungary	68.6	89.2	97.1	73.5	0.0	0.0	0.0	37.2
Iceland	86.9	90.9	92.5	0.1	0.0	0.0	0.3	98.8
Ireland	2.9	2.0	1.2	0.0	0.3	49.0	99.4	101.2
Italy	97.6	97.3	97.4	2.8	0.0	0.0	2.1	97.5
Japan	59.8	94.9	96.1	0.0	0.0	0.0	0.0	102.1
Korea	9.7	25.1	43.2	0.0	0.0	0.0	1.1	92.4
Luxembourg	37.5	94.3	91.2	3.4	0.1	0.2	2.8	91.3
Mexico	14.6	57.2	80.8	0.9	0.0	0.0	9.9	102.9
Netherlands	0.1	99.5	98.5	0.0	0.0	0.0	0.0	99.5
New Zealand	80.5	93.1	2.7	0.0	0.0	0.0	96.4	99.1
Norway	70.9	78.1	81.2	1.1	0.0	0.0	0.0	99.3
Poland	23.3	33.3	40.9	96.7	0.0	0.0	0.0	0.7
Portugal	55.9	72.2	81.6	3.2	0.0	0.0	0.0	101.4
Slovak Republic	56.1	70.3	81.5	34.2	0.0	0.0	0.0	m
Spain	79.6	93.5	100.5	0.1	0.0	0.0	0.0	101.5
Sweden	68.0	72.8	75.8	96.4	0.0	0.0	0.0	4.3
Switzerland	7.0	30.7	83.1	65.1	0.1	0.3	0.7	35.4
Turkey	0.0	0.0	18.9	0.0	0.0	0.0	5.5	86.1
United Kingdom	53.9	100.0	0.1	0.0	0.0	0.0	99.9	98.9
United States	36.0	63.6	74.2	10.6	0.0	0.0	6.0	88.3

m: missing data.

1. The data refer to pre-primary education, which is limited to organised centre-based programmes designed to foster learning and emotional and social development in children from 3 to compulsory school age. Day care, play groups and home-based structured and developmental activities may not be included in these data. In some countries, the net enrolment rate at age 6 exceeds 100% due to different reference dates for counting enrolments in various programmes.

Source: OECD (2002).

Data for Figure 1.2

Expenditure on pre-primary education as a percentage of GDP, 1999

Direct and indirect expenditure on educational institutions from public and private sources

Australia	0.09		Luxembourg	m
Austria	0.53		Mexico	0.50
Belgium[1]	0.48		Netherlands	0.36
Canada	0.25		New Zealand[1]	0.19
Czech Republic	0.53		Norway	0.80
Denmark	0.78		Poland[1]	0.44
Finland	0.40		Portugal	0.29
France	0.68		Slovak Republic	0.52
Germany	0.57		Spain	0.42
Greece	x		Sweden	0.58
Hungary	0.79		Switzerland	0.20
Iceland	m		Turkey	m
Ireland	n		United Kingdom	0.42
Italy	0.43		United States	0.39
Japan	0.18			
Korea	0.15		Country mean	0.44
			OECD total	0.39

m: missing data.
n: magnitude is either negligible or zero.
x: indicates that data are included in another level of education.

1. Including only direct public expenditure on educational institutions.

Source: OECD (2002).

chapter 2

IMPROVING BOTH QUALITY AND EQUITY: INSIGHTS FROM PISA 2000

▼

SUMMARY

The OECD Programme for International Student Assessment (PISA) produced the results of its first international survey of 15-year-olds in 2001. As well as describing considerable differences in student performance across and within countries, the results start to give valuable insights relevant for the formulation of educational policy. In particular, the analyses in this chapter suggest that:

– Quality and equity do not have to be seen as competing policy objectives. A number of countries achieved high overall performance standards alongside a relatively narrow distribution of student results.

– While spending on schools is important for the provision of high-quality schooling, spending alone does not guarantee better outcomes. Some countries achieved high performance with relatively limited resources, and vice versa.

– Building student engagement with reading, and with school more generally, may help lift overall performance and reduce the influence of coming from a relatively disadvantaged home background. Strikingly, being more enthusiastic about reading and a frequent reader was more of an advantage, on its own, than having well-educated parents in good jobs.

– School practices appear to make a difference: students tend to perform better in schools characterised by high expectations, the enjoyment of learning, a strong disciplinary climate, and good teacher-student relations.

– Countries that combine a clear focus on student performance with greater levels of school autonomy tend to perform better on average, and greater school autonomy is not necessarily associated with larger variation in school performance.

– Overall performance appears to be higher, and variation among students narrower, in systems with a lesser degree of differentiation between different types of schools.

1. INTRODUCTION

How well do school systems perform in providing all young people with a solid foundation of knowledge and skills, and in preparing them for life and learning beyond school? Parents, students, the public and those who manage education systems need to know the answers to such questions.

Many national education systems regularly monitor the outcomes of student learning, with methods ranging from broad assessments of samples of students up to high-stakes individual and subject-specific examinations. Comparative international analyses can extend and enrich the picture by providing a larger context within which to interpret national results. They can show countries their areas of relative strength and weakness, and help them to monitor progress and raise aspirations. They can also provide directions for national policy, for schools' curriculum and instructional efforts, and for students' learning.

Since 1997, the OECD Member countries have been building on earlier international work to establish a comparative framework to assess how well their school systems meet core objectives. The result is the OECD Programme for International Student Assessment (PISA), the most comprehensive exercise to date

---

Box 2.1 PISA 2000 – an internationally standardised assessment of 15-year-olds

Sample size

More than a quarter of a million students, representing almost 17 million 15-year-olds enrolled in the schools of the 32 participating countries, were assessed in 2000. Another 13 countries are administering the same assessment during 2002.

Content

- PISA 2000 covered three "domains": reading literacy; mathematical literacy; and scientific literacy. In this first survey the main focus was on reading literacy.

- PISA 2000 looked at young people's ability to use their knowledge and skills in order to meet real-life challenges, rather than how well they had mastered a specific school curriculum. The emphasis was on the mastery of processes, the understanding of concepts, and their application to solving problems.

Methods

- Pencil-and-paper assessments, lasting two hours for each student.

- A combination of multiple-choice questions and questions that required students to construct their own answers. Questions were typically organised in units based on a passage describing a real-life situation.

- A total of seven hours of assessment items was included, with different students taking different combinations of the assessment items in their two hours.

- Students answered a background questionnaire that took about 30 minutes to complete and, in 25 countries, completed questionnaires on learning and study practices as well as familiarity with computers.

- School principals completed a questionnaire about their school.

- An important limitation of PISA 2000 is that no information was collected from teachers. Such data are difficult to collect and interpret as students in the PISA samples are generally taught by a number of different teachers. The issue of collecting data from teachers is under continuing investigation.

Future assessments

PISA will continue in three-year cycles. In 2003, the main focus will be on mathematics, and in 2006 on science. The assessment of cross-curricular competencies is being progressively integrated into PISA, beginning with an assessment of problem-solving skills in 2003.

Further information

Details on the design of PISA 2000 and the international results are provided in *Knowledge and Skills for Life – First Results from* PISA 2000 (OECD, 2001a). Further information is available from *www.pisa.oecd.org*

---

aimed at the assessment of learning outcomes within an international comparative perspective. Box 2.1 provides an overview of the first PISA survey of student knowledge and skills, which took place in 2000.

This chapter explores some of the factors that the PISA 2000 results suggest are associated with high quality learning outcomes. It begins by briefly summarising the performance of countries in the PISA assessment, both in terms of the knowledge and skills which 15-year-olds display in key areas, and the extent to which education systems deliver equitable learning outcomes. The chapter then investigates characteristics of schools and school systems that are associated with strong and equitable performance. In particular, it seeks to identify those characteristics that policy makers can do something about.

2. EVIDENCE ON THE QUALITY AND EQUITY OF STUDENT PERFORMANCE

2.1 Performance levels among 15-year-olds

First results from PISA 2000 were published in 2001, showing how well 15-year-olds in OECD and other countries can apply knowledge and skills in key subject areas. The results revealed wide differences not just among countries, but also among schools and students within countries.[1]

Box 2.2 summarises the five levels of reading literacy proficiency developed in PISA 2000. In Australia, Canada, Finland, New Zealand and the United Kingdom, more than 15% of students displayed the highest level of reading proficiency (Level 5), showing that they are capable of completing sophisticated reading tasks (see Figure 2.1). By contrast, this proportion was 5% or less in Brazil, Greece, Latvia, Luxembourg, Mexico, Portugal, the Russian Federation and Spain.

Students with literacy skills at or below Level 1 may not only encounter difficulties in their initial transition from education to work, but may also fail to benefit fully from further education and learning opportunities throughout life. In Finland and Korea, only around 5% of students perform at Level 1, and less than 2% below it, but these countries are exceptions. In all of the other countries 10% or more of students perform at or below Level 1.

Box 2.2 Reading literacy proficiency levels in PISA 2000

Level 5 (*over 625 points*): students are capable of sophisticated reading tasks, such as: managing information that is difficult to find in unfamiliar texts; showing detailed understanding and inferring which information is relevant to the task; being able to evaluate critically and build hypotheses; drawing on specialised knowledge; and accommodating concepts that may be contrary to expectations.

Level 4 (*553 to 625 points*): students are capable of difficult reading tasks, such as locating embedded information, construing meaning from nuances of language, and critically evaluating a text.

Level 3 (*481-552 points*): students are capable of reading tasks of moderate complexity, such as locating multiple pieces of information, drawing links between different parts of the text, and relating it to everyday knowledge.

Level 2 (*408-480 points*): students are capable of basic reading tasks, such as locating straightforward information, making low-level inferences of various types, deciding what a well-defined part of the text means, and using some outside knowledge to understand it.

Level 1 (*335-407 points*): students are capable of only the least complex reading tasks, such as locating a single piece of information, identifying the main theme of a text, or making a simple connection with everyday knowledge.

Below Level 1 (*below 335 points*): students are not able to show routinely the most basic type of knowledge and skills that PISA seeks to measure. These students may have serious difficulties in using reading literacy as an effective tool to advance and extend their knowledge and skills in other areas.

Figure 2.1 Percentage of students performing at each proficiency level on the PISA reading literacy scale, and the relative standing of countries, PISA 2000

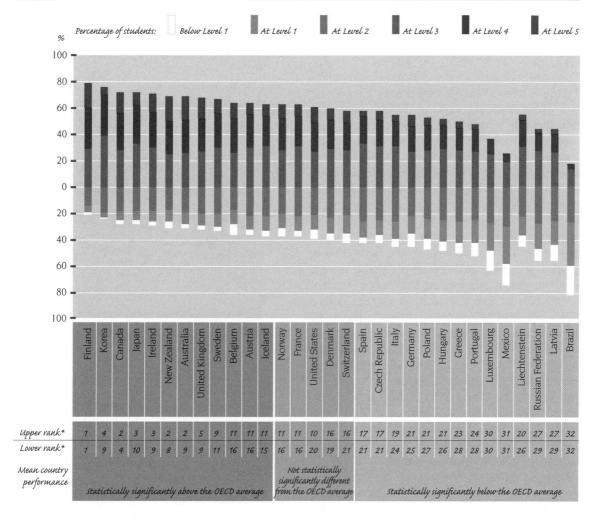

* Because data are based on samples, it is not possible to report exact rank order positions for countries. However, it is possible to report the range of rank order positions within which the country mean lies with 95% likelihood. Data for the Netherlands were not included because the response rate was too low to ensure comparability.

Source: OECD PISA database at *www.pisa.oecd.org* ....

Data for Figure 2.1, p. 58.

Twelve countries recorded at least 20% of students at Level 1 literacy or below. The existence of a significant minority of students who, at age 15, lack the foundation of literacy skills needed for further learning, is of concern to those seeking to make lifelong learning a reality for all.

It is possible to summarise the performance of students in each country by computing a mean score across all student groups,[2] and then to

1. For most countries, performance in PISA is similar across the areas of reading, mathematical and scientific literacy. This chapter mainly focuses on student performance in reading literacy. It also concentrates on the 28 OECD countries that took part in PISA 2000. Further details on performance in all three areas, and in the four non-OECD countries in PISA 2000, are provided in OECD (2001*a*).

2. The scale that is used for this purpose was established such that the average score across OECD countries is 500, with about two-thirds of students across OECD countries scoring between 400 and 600 points.

IMPROVING BOTH QUALITY AND EQUITY:
INSIGHTS FROM PISA 2000

assess the relative standing of countries in the international comparison on this measure. The rank order position of each country for student performance in reading literacy is also shown in Figure 2.1.

For some countries, the results displayed in Figure 2.1 were deeply disappointing, showing that their students' average performance lags considerably behind that of other countries, and sometimes despite high investments in schooling. Overall, however, the PISA 2000 results are encouraging. The performance of countries such as Finland and Korea reveals that excellence in schooling is attainable, and at reasonable cost.

Figure 2.2 compares the money that countries spend per student, on average, from the beginning of primary education up to the age of 15, with average student performance.[3] As expenditure per student on schools increases, so also, on average, does a country's mean performance.[4] However, deviations from the trend line suggest that moderate spending per student is not necessarily associated with poor student performance. For example, Ireland and Korea are among the best performing countries, but spend less than US$35 000 per student up to the age of 15 years, well below the OECD average of US$45 000. Conversely, Italy spends almost US$60 000 per student but performs significantly below the OECD average. Figure 2.2 therefore suggests that, as much as spending on schools is necessary for the provision of high-quality schooling, spending alone does not guarantee better outcomes. This chapter explores some of the other factors that seem to be important.

2.2 Social distribution of learning outcomes

Students come from a variety of social and cultural backgrounds. As a result, schools need to provide appropriate and equitable opportunities for a diverse student body. The relative success with which they do so is another important criterion for judging performance. Identifying the characteristics of the students who perform poorly can also help educators and policy makers determine priorities for policy intervention. Similarly, identifying the characteristics of students who perform well can assist policy makers to promote high levels of performance across-the-board.

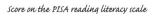

Figure 2.2 Student performance on the PISA reading literacy scale and expenditure per student, OECD countries

Relationship between the average performance on the PISA reading literacy scale and cumulative expenditure on educational institutions from age 6 up to age 15 in US$, converted using purchasing power parities (PPP)

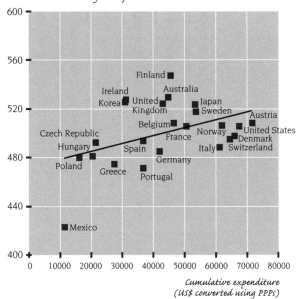

Score on the PISA reading literacy scale

Cumulative expenditure (US$ converted using PPPs)

Source: OECD PISA database at *www.pisa.oecd.org*; OECD (2001b). ....
Data for Figure 2.2, p. 59.

The report *Knowledge and Skills for Life – First Results from* PISA 2000 (OECD, 2001a) shows that poor performance in school does not automatically follow from a disadvantaged home background. However, home background remains one of the most powerful factors influencing performance. The report shows, in particular, that:

3. Spending per student is approximated by multiplying public and private expenditure on educational institutions per student in 1998 at each level of education by the theoretical duration of education at the respective level, up to the age of 15. Expenditure on schooling is expressed in US$ using purchasing power parities (PPP). The PPP exchange rates equalise the purchasing power of different currencies. This means that comparisons between countries reflect only differences in the volume of goods and services purchased.

4. Expenditure per student explains 19% of the variation between countries in mean performance on the reading literacy scale. The correlation for the overall relationship is 0.44.

– Parental occupational status, which is often closely interrelated with other attributes of socio-economic status, has a strong association with student performance. The average performance gap between students in the top quarter of PISA's index of occupational status (whose parents have occupations like medicine, university teaching and law) and those in the bottom quarter (occupations such as small-scale farming, truck-driving, and serving in restaurants), amounts to more than an entire proficiency level in reading literacy. In Germany, the difference is particularly striking. Students whose parents have the highest-status jobs score on average about as well as the average student in Finland, the best-performing country in PISA 2000; German students whose parents have the lowest-status jobs score about the same, on average, as students in Mexico, the OECD country with the lowest average performance in PISA.

– Possessions and activities related to "classical" culture also tend to be closely related to performance.[5] The possession of the kind of cultural capital on which school curricula often tend to build, and which examinations and tests assess, appears closely related to student reading scores. The results of PISA 2000 also suggest that educational success may be related to patterns of communication between parents and children.

– Family wealth is also associated with higher levels of performance, although the relationship appears to be weaker than that of the other home background factors examined here.[6]

– Students who were born outside the country, as well as those who were born inside the country but have foreign-born parents tend, in most countries, to score much lower than other students, even after accounting for their other characteristics. The same is true for students whose language is different from the language of instruction. In both cases, however, the performance gap varies widely across countries.

Nevertheless, the PISA 2000 results show that while social background is a powerful influence on learning outcomes, it plays a lesser role in some countries than in others. The policy goal must be to provide opportunities for all students to achieve their full potential. PISA 2000 suggests that this goal can be achieved.

3. IS THERE A TRADE-OFF BETWEEN QUALITY AND EQUITY?

Achieving an equitable distribution of learning outcomes without losing high performance standards represents a significant challenge. Analyses at the national level have often been discouraging: schools have appeared to make little difference in overcoming the effects of disadvantaged home backgrounds. As well, it has sometimes been argued that if school systems become more inclusive – for example, by increasing the proportion of young people who complete secondary school – then quality is bound to suffer. The international evidence from PISA 2000 is more encouraging. First of all, it is evident that wide disparities in student performance are not a necessary condition for a country to attain a high level of overall performance. Furthermore, while all countries show that students with more advantaged home backgrounds tend to have higher PISA scores, some countries demonstrate that high average quality and equality of outcomes among students from different backgrounds can go together. Figure 2.3 contrasts average performance in PISA 2000 in reading literacy – as shown

5. "Classical" cultural activities were measured through self-reports on how often students had participated in the following activities during the preceding year: visited a museum or art gallery; attended an opera, ballet or classical symphony concert; and watched live theatre. "Classical" cultural possessions in the family home were measured through students' reports on the availability of the following items in their home: classical literature (examples were given); books of poetry; and works of art (examples were given).

6. Family wealth was derived from students' reports on: a) the availability, in their home, of a dishwasher, a room of their own, educational software, and a link to the Internet; and b) the number of cellular phones, television sets, computers, motor cars and bathrooms at home. Home educational resources were derived from students' reports on the availability and number of the following items in their home: a dictionary; a quiet place to study; a desk for study; textbooks; and calculators.

IMPROVING BOTH QUALITY AND EQUITY:
INSIGHTS FROM PISA 2000

on the vertical axis – with the impact of family background on student performance – as shown on the horizontal axis.[7]

Canada, Finland, Iceland, Japan, Korea and Sweden all display above-average levels of student performance in reading literacy and, at the same time, a below-average impact of economic, social and cultural status on student performance. Conversely, average performance in reading literacy in the Czech Republic, Germany, Hungary, Luxembourg and Switzerland is below the OECD average while, at the same time, these countries display above-average disparities between

students from advantaged and disadvantaged family backgrounds.[8]

An important finding of PISA 2000 is thus that countries differ not just in their overall performance, but also in the extent to which they are able to close the performance gap between students from different social backgrounds. PISA 2000 suggests that maximising overall performance and securing similar levels of performance among students from different social backgrounds can be achieved simultaneously. The results suggest that quality and equity need not be considered as competing policy objectives.

Figure 2.3 Performance in reading and the impact of family background, OECD countries, PISA 2000

Relationship between the average performance of OECD countries on the PISA reading literacy scale and the socio-economic distribution of student performance

Score on the PISA reading literacy scale

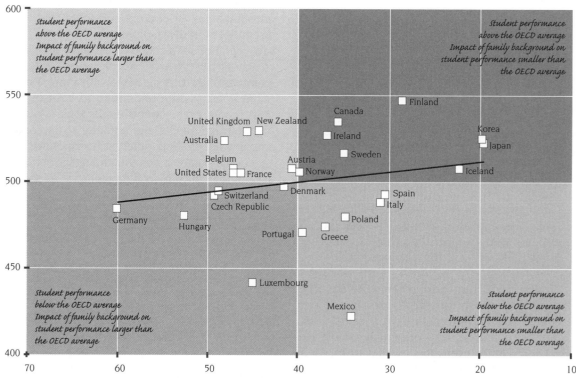

Score point difference associated with one unit on the PISA index of economic, cultural and social status

Note: The mean reading performance in five countries is not statistically different from the OECD average: Denmark, France, Norway, Switzerland and the United States. The socio-economic distribution of student performance in eight countries is not statistically different from the OECD average: Austria, Denmark, Greece, Ireland, New Zealand, Norway, Poland and Portugal.

For the definition of the PISA index of economic, social and cultural status, see OECD (2001*a*).

Source: OECD PISA database at *www.pisa.oecd.org* --

Data for Figure 2.3, p. 59.

Education Policy Analysis

4. POINTERS FOR POLICY

The high and equitable performance standards achieved by some countries set ambitious goals for others. The question is what they can learn from the results to help students to achieve more, teachers to teach better, and schools to be more effective. PISA 2000 does not show which policies or practices *cause* success, but it does allow us to observe some common characteristics of high-performing students, schools and systems. PISA cannot, on its own, provide clear-cut answers as to why the countries performed so differently, or definitive guidance to the policy directions that countries should take. However, analyses of the wide range of student and school background data collected by PISA 2000 can provide pointers to stimulate and inform national debate, as well as guide future work.

4.1 Strengthening student engagement

Developing the predisposition of students to engage with learning and the capacity to do so effectively are important objectives, especially with an eye to fostering lifelong learning. Students who leave school with the capacity to set their own learning goals, and with a sense that they can reach those goals, are potential learners for life.

In PISA 2000, students' engagement with learning was measured by their engagement in reading, as well as by their broader engagement with school. Reading engagement was measured through a combination of the student's reading habits and attitudes.[9] A comparison of countries on this index shows that students' engagement in reading is clearly linked with reading proficiency, although the data do not allow one to discern in which direction this relationship operates and to what extent other, non-measured factors are at play. In all countries, students who are more engaged in reading score, on average, better.[10]

Table 2.1 shows, not surprisingly, that the country with the highest level of engagement in reading is the one with the highest average reading scores, Finland, in which students' average score on the index of engagement is 0.46. Other countries where the level of engagement in reading is high

are Denmark (0.26), Iceland (0.27), Japan (0.20) and Korea (0.21). By comparison, countries where the level of engagement is relatively low are Belgium (-0.28), Germany (-0.26), Ireland (-0.20), Luxembourg (-0.19) and Spain (-0.23). To some extent the differences among country means on the index may represent cultural differences in student responses to the questions through which engagement was captured. Ireland is an example of a high-performing country in which there is a strong within-country relationship between student engagement and reading performance, but where there is a relatively low country average on the engagement index.

In addition to the strong association between student performance in reading literacy and engagement in reading within countries, the analysis also

---

7. To capture a student's family and home background, an index of economic, social and cultural status was created on the basis of students' reports on the following background characteristics: the occupation of the parents; the highest level of education of the student's parents; an index of family wealth; an index of home educational resources; and an index of cultural possessions in the family home. Details of these measures are provided in OECD (2002*a*).

8. In such a comparison, the spread of social background characteristics in the population needs to be taken into consideration, as social equity in student learning outcomes may be more difficult to obtain in countries with large social disparities in the population. To shed light on this, the last column in the data table for Figure 2.3 (see p. 59) shows the difference between the 95th and 5th percentiles of the student distribution on the PISA index of economic, cultural and social status, which illustrates the extent of socio-economic differences in the families of 15-year-olds in each country. It is noteworthy that the cross-country correlation between this measure and the socio-economic differences in PISA scores is small and not statistically significant, suggesting that the results cannot be explained with the spread of social background characteristics as measured by PISA.

9. Specifically, students were asked to rate how frequently they read different kinds of material and how much time they invest in reading for enjoyment. Both aspects were combined into an index, in which the engagement level for the average OECD student is set at zero, and two-thirds of students score between +1 and -1. Thus a positive or negative score does not indicate positive or negative engagement in reading, but shows whether students are more or less engaged than the average for other students in OECD countries.

10. The within-country correlation between reading performance and engagement averages 0.38 in OECD countries, and the cross-country correlation between mean reading performance and mean engagement is 0.27.

Table 2.1 Reading performance and engagement in reading, OECD countries

	Performance on the PISA reading literacy scale		PISA index of engagement in reading[1]		Correlation between the PISA index of engagement in reading and proficiency on the PISA reading literacy scale	
	Mean score	S.E.	Mean index	S.E.		
Australia	528	(3.5)	-0.04	(0.03)	0.42	-(0.02)
Austria	507	(2.4)	-0.08	(0.03)	0.41	-(0.02)
Belgium	507	(3.6)	-0.28	(0.02)	0.36	-(0.02)
Canada	534	(1.6)	0.01	(0.01)	0.40	-(0.01)
Czech Republic	492	(2.4)	0.02	(0.02)	0.42	-(0.01)
Denmark	497	(2.4)	0.26	(0.02)	0.43	-(0.02)
Finland	546	(2.6)	0.46	(0.02)	0.48	-(0.01)
France	505	(2.7)	-0.18	(0.02)	0.35	-(0.01)
Germany	484	(2.5)	-0.26	(0.02)	0.41	-(0.02)
Greece	474	(5.0)	-0.09	(0.02)	0.25	-(0.02)
Hungary	480	(4.0)	0.03	(0.02)	0.41	-(0.02)
Iceland	507	(1.5)	0.27	(0.01)	0.45	-(0.02)
Ireland	527	(3.2)	-0.20	(0.02)	0.39	-(0.02)
Italy	487	(2.9)	-0.08	(0.02)	0.30	-(0.02)
Japan	522	(5.2)	0.20	(0.03)	0.32	-(0.01)
Korea	525	(2.4)	0.21	(0.02)	0.35	-(0.01)
Luxembourg	441	(1.6)	-0.19	(0.02)	0.25	-(0.02)
Mexico	422	(3.3)	0.07	(0.01)	0.24	-(0.02)
New Zealand	529	(2.8)	0.05	(0.02)	0.35	-(0.02)
Norway	505	(2.8)	0.09	(0.02)	0.45	-(0.02)
Poland	479	(4.5)	-0.10	(0.02)	0.28	-(0.02)
Portugal	470	(4.5)	0.13	(0.02)	0.32	-(0.02)
Spain	493	(2.7)	-0.23	(0.02)	0.38	-(0.01)
Sweden	516	(2.2)	0.14	(0.02)	0.45	-(0.02)
Switzerland	494	(4.3)	0.00	(0.01)	0.46	-(0.02)
United Kingdom	523	(2.6)	-0.10	(0.02)	0.37	-(0.02)
United States	504	(7.1)	-0.14	(0.03)	0.31	-(0.02)
OECD average	**500**		**0.00**		**0.38**	
Netherlands[2]			-0.2	(0.04)	0.38	-(0.02)

1. For a definition of this index, see footnote 9. Note that the definition of this index differs slightly from the index used in OECD (2001*a*).

2. Response rate is too low to ensure comparability.

Source: OECD PISA database at *www.pisa.oecd.org*; OECD (2001*a*).

suggests that student engagement in reading may be an important factor that can offset social disadvantage. In order to examine this issue, students were classified in terms of whether they reported low, medium or high engagement in reading, and whether their parents had low, medium or high occupational status. For this purpose, "medium" refers in each case to the middle half of students, and "low" and "high" refer to the top and bottom quarters respectively.

Students who are less engaged readers tend to be more numerous among the group of students whose parents have the lowest occupational status. Highly engaged students are more numerous among the group of students whose parents have the highest occupational status. However, PISA also shows that there are students from disadvantaged family backgrounds who are highly engaged in reading, as well as students from more privileged backgrounds who are among the least engaged readers (Table 2.2).

Table 2.3 records how these groups of students are distributed in terms of their reading literacy performance. Not surprisingly, students who have parents with the highest occupational status and who are highly engaged in reading obtain the best average scores on the reading literacy scale (583). Students who have parents with the lowest occupational status and who are the least engaged in reading achieved the lowest average score (423). However, perhaps most importantly, students who are highly engaged readers and whose parents have the lowest occupational status achieved significantly higher average reading scores (540) than students whose parents have the highest occupational status but who are poorly engaged in reading (491). Furthermore, these highly engaged students whose parents have low occupational status performed as well on average as those students who are in the middle engagement group but whose parents have high-status occupations. That is to say, coming from a higher-status home background is less of an advantage, on its own, than being more highly engaged in reading.

Students who are highly engaged in reading achieve reading literacy scores which, on average, are significantly above the international mean (500), whatever their family background. Conversely, students who are poorly engaged in reading

obtained scores below the international mean, regardless of their parents' occupational status. Within each grouping of occupational status, students who are in the group of least engaged readers attain average reading literacy scores which are from 85 to 117 points lower than those who are in the highly engaged reading group (see Table 2.3). The largest such difference is seen among students whose parents have the lowest-status occupations.

These findings are of paramount importance from an educational perspective. Although the data do not show in which direction the relationship operates, one interpretation is that building student engagement with reading can play an important role in reducing the gap between the reading performance of students coming from different family backgrounds. Achieving this objective will also serve other important educational goals since reading is a fundamental skill required across the curriculum.

The patterns shown for engagement in reading are largely mirrored in students' broader engagement with school, although the relationship differs

Table 2.2 Expected and observed percentages of students classified by the PISA index of engagement in reading and the PISA index of occupational status, 2000

PISA index of occupational status	Low engagement		Medium engagement		High engagement	
	"Expected"	Observed	"Expected"	Observed	"Expected"	Observed
Low	6.3	7.6	12.3	12.6	6.3	4.9
Medium	12.3	12.9	25.0	25.1	12.3	12.0
High	6.3	4.5	12.3	12.3	6.3	8.2
Total	**25.0**	**25.0**	**50.0**	**50.0**	**25.0**	**25.0**

Note: The "expected" percentage of students in a given category is simply the nominal percentage obtained from allocating one-quarter of the "low" and "high" students on each variable, and one-half of the "medium" students, respectively, to the category concerned. The "observed" percentage is the actual percentage of students in each category as revealed by the PISA results.

Source: OECD PISA database at *www.pisa.oecd.org* ....

Table 2.3 Reading performance of students classified by the PISA index of engagement in reading and the PISA index of occupational status, 2000

PISA index of occupational status	Low engagement	Medium engagement	High engagement
Low	423	467	540
Medium	463	506	548
High	491	540	583

Source: OECD PISA database at *www.pisa.oecd.org* ....

across countries. The evidence from PISA 2000 suggests that those students who are engaged in school perform better than those who are not. In almost all countries, students who report that school is a place where they want to go perform better than those who do not. Across the OECD, an average of 87% of students report that school is a place where they make friends easily, and three-quarters say that school is a place where they feel they belong, the proportion ranging from around 50% or less in France and Spain to 88% in Hungary and Mexico. By contrast, there is a small but significant group of students for whom school is a difficult social environment. On average, across the OECD, 13% of students report that school is a place where they feel awkward and out of place (for country data see OECD, 2001a).

The data on engagement in school do not establish a causal relationship with student performance. There are other factors that influence both performance and attitudes towards school. In addition, doing well at school might cause students to like it more, rather than vice versa. However, it is unsatisfactory that a significant minority of students – and in some cases even a majority – display a lack of engagement, and negative attitudes towards school. It is hard to imagine that schools can achieve good results unless students are positively engaged. Furthermore, students who are disaffected with school may also be less likely to engage in learning activities in later life.

Schools and education systems need to aim at lifting *both* performance and engagement, in order to increase average performance and to ensure an equitable distribution of learning outcomes. For example, teachers need to provide each student with the skills to be a good reader, as well as interesting the student in being a good reader. If these mutually reinforcing goals can be achieved, a more secure foundation for lifelong learning will have been established for students from all backgrounds.

4.2 Shifting the focus to learning outcomes

The PISA 2000 results confirm a range of other research which suggests that students perform best in a positive learning environment that is oriented towards results. PISA 2000 indicates that students and schools perform better in a climate character-

ised by high expectations and the readiness to invest effort, the enjoyment of learning, a strong disciplinary climate, and good teacher-student relations. Among these aspects, students' perception of teacher-student relations and classroom disciplinary climate have the strongest relationships with student performance, across countries.[11] Performance orientation, which was measured by students' perceptions of the extent to which teachers emphasise academic performance and place high demands on students, is also positively related to performance, but less strongly so. Students also perform better where principals report a more positive school climate, higher teacher morale, and a greater degree of school autonomy.[12]

Many of the countries that performed well in PISA 2000 have been progressively shifting education policy and practice away from a focus on inputs – the resources, structures and content of schooling – and towards a focus on learning outcomes. Perhaps not surprisingly therefore, PISA 2000 shows that schools in such countries often have greater freedom to organise their learning environment and the range of subjects that they offer, and to administer the resources allocated to them.

Devolving more decision-making authority to schools has been a key strategy in many countries since the early 1980s. School-based management is intended to increase creativity and responsiveness to local needs. This involves enhancing the decision-making responsibility and accountability of principals and, in some cases, the management responsibilities of teachers or department heads.

In order to gauge the extent to which school staff have a say in decisions relating to school policy and management, principals in PISA 2000 were asked to report whether teachers, department heads, the principal, an appointed or elected board, or education authorities, had the main responsibility for a wide range of aspects of schooling. The results are summarised in Figure 2.4 (see also data table for Figure 2.4 at end of the chapter).

According to school principals, schools in most countries appear to have little say in the establishment of teachers' starting salaries and in determining teachers' salary increases. In all countries other than

Figure 2.4 Percentage of students enrolled in schools which have at least some responsibility for the following aspects of school policy and management, OECD countries, PISA 2000 (each country represented by a dot)

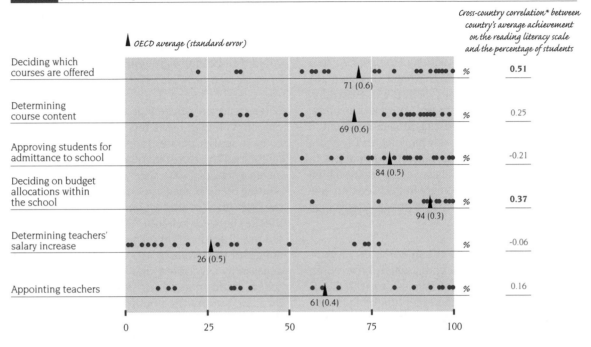

* Statistically significant correlations are shown in bold.

Source: OECD PISA database at www.pisa.oecd.org

Data for Figure 2.4, pp. 60-61.

the Czech Republic, Greece, the Netherlands, the United Kingdom and the United States, two-thirds or more of 15-year-olds are enrolled in schools whose principals report that schools have no responsibility for the establishment of teachers' starting salaries. The scope to reward teachers financially, once they have been hired, is also limited. Only in the Czech Republic, Greece, Sweden, the United Kingdom and the United States are more than two-thirds of the students enrolled in schools which have some responsibility for determining teachers' salary increases.

There appears to be greater flexibility for schools with regard to the appointment and dismissal of teachers. Germany and Italy are the only countries in which about 90% or more of 15-year-olds are enrolled in schools whose principals report that the school has no responsibility in these matters. Conversely, in Belgium, the Czech Republic, Denmark, Iceland, Sweden, Switzerland, the United Kingdom and the United States, at least 93% of students attend schools that have some responsibility for the appointment of teachers (the

OECD average is 61%). In the majority of countries, principals tend to report a more prominent role for the school in appointing teachers than in dismissing them, the largest differences being found in Canada and Denmark (21 and 40 percentage points, respectively). In Belgium, the Czech Republic, Hungary, Iceland, the Netherlands, New Zealand, and the United States, more than 95%

11. The average difference between the reading literacy scores of students who report these characteristics as more favourable or less favourable (separated by one standard deviation in the international distribution of students ranked according to each characteristic), is 18 points in the case of student-teacher relations and 10 in the case of disciplinary climate (see OECD, 2001a).

12. An increase of one unit on the respective PISA indices (corresponding to one international standard deviation) is associated with gains on the reading literacy scale of about 6, 2 and 5 points, respectively (see OECD, 2001a). When interpreting such results, it should be noted that many factors influencing student performance, in particular those related to teachers and teaching, were not directly measured in PISA 2000. The results reported here are therefore likely to understate the impact of such factors.

of the students are enrolled in schools whose principals report having some say in the dismissal of teachers (the OECD average is 54%).

There is variation also with regard to the roles that schools play in the formulation of budgets, Austria and Germany reporting the least involvement of schools with this task. Schools in Australia, Belgium, Italy, Luxembourg, the Netherlands, New Zealand, the United Kingdom and the United States have a comparatively high degree of school autonomy with regard to budget formulation. In most countries, principals generally report a high degree of school involvement in decisions on how money is spent within schools (the OECD average is 94%).

In all OECD countries, the majority of 15-year-olds are enrolled in schools which have some responsibility for student admissions (the OECD average is 84%). With the exception of Germany, Italy and Switzerland, the majority of 15-year-olds are also enrolled in schools that play a role in deciding on the courses offered (the OECD average is 71%). Finally, most principals (the OECD average is around 90%) report that disciplinary policies, assessment policies and choice of textbooks are school responsibilities.

Does the distribution of decision-making responsibilities affect student performance? In some countries, most notably Australia, Austria, Canada, Ireland, Spain and Switzerland the relationship between school autonomy and student performance is strong and significant, even when other school characteristics are held constant.[13] In other countries, the association between the different aspects of school autonomy and student performance *within* the country tends to be weaker, often because legislation specifies the distribution of decision-making responsibilities so that there is little variation among schools. When looking *across* countries, however, PISA 2000 suggests that in those countries in which principals report, on average, a higher degree of school autonomy with regard to choice of courses, the average performance in reading literacy tends to be higher than in other countries. The cross-country relationship is summarised by the country-level correlations shown in Figure 2.4.[14] The picture is similar, though less pronounced, for other aspects of school autonomy, including the relationship between mean performance and the degree of school autonomy in budget allocation. This finding cannot, of course, be interpreted in a causal sense as, for example, school autonomy and performance could well be mutually reinforcing or influenced by other factors.

While countries with greater levels of school autonomy in particular areas tend to perform better, a concern is that greater independence of schools might lead to greater inequalities in the performance of schools. One way to examine this is by relating the PISA measures of school autonomy to the proportion of student performance differences that lies between schools.[15] This comparison does not reveal a consistent relationship, and therefore suggests that greater school autonomy is not necessarily associated with greater disparities in school performance. For example, Finland and Sweden, among the countries with the highest degree of school autonomy on many of the measures used in PISA 2000 display, together with Iceland, the smallest performance differences among schools.

As a counterpart to more autonomy, schools in the better performing countries also tend to be responsible for addressing the needs of a diverse student population. They rarely have the option to transfer students to educational streams or school types with lower performance requirements, options that often exist in lower performing countries. These aspects are examined more closely in the next section.

---

13. For these countries, the effect size of the relationship between the PISA index of school autonomy and student performance on the reading literacy scale is between 8 and 38 score points on the PISA reading literacy scale (see OECD, 2001a).

14. It should be noted that the analysis is subject to the limitation that there were 32 countries from which PISA students were sampled in 2000. While this number of countries is an advance over most previous comparative analyses, it remains small. Consequently, effects need to be fairly strong to be detectable by conventional statistical standards. Expressed as a bivariate correlation, only coefficients of 0.30 or higher will be statistically significant.

15. The performance differences between schools are indicated in Figure 2.5 and its supporting data table.

4.3 Securing consistent standards for schools

Some countries have non-selective school systems in which all schools provide similar opportunities for learning and need to cater for the full range of student performance. Other countries respond to diversity by forming groups of students of similar levels of performance through selection either within or between schools, with the aim of serving students according to their respective ability levels and needs. How do such policies and practices affect actual student performance and the ways in which family background influences student success?

Figure 2.5 shows considerable differences in the extent to which the reading literacy skills of 15-year-olds vary within each country. The length of the bars

---

Figure 2.5 Variations in reading literacy performance between and within schools, OECD countries, PISA 2000

Expressed as a percentage of the average variation in student performance in OECD countries

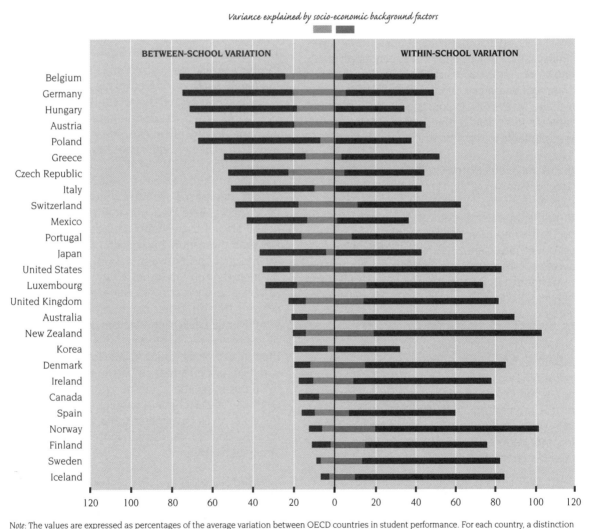

Variance explained by socio-economic background factors

Note: The values are expressed as percentages of the average variation between OECD countries in student performance. For each country, a distinction is made between how much of this variation can be accounted for by the different results of each school (to the left of the central line) and how much is to do with a range of student results within each school (to the right of the central line). The length of each segment is relative to the total variation in all OECD countries, which is set at 100. A bar longer than 100 in a segment on the horizontal axis indicates that variation in student performance is greater in that country than in a typical OECD country. A value smaller than 100 indicates below-average variation in student performance. The shading on the bars in each segment at the middle part of the chart indicates the proportion of variation explained by socio-economic background factors. Owing to the sampling methods used in Japan, the between-school variation in Japan includes variation between classes within schools.

Source: OECD PISA database at *www.pisa.oecd.org* ....

Data for Figure 2.5, p. 62.

indicates the total observed variation in student performance in reading literacy. For each country, a distinction is made between how much of this variation can be accounted for by the different results of each school and how much is to do with a range of student results within each school. The length of bars to the left of the central line shows between-school differences; to the right are within-school differences. Note that the numbers on each segment are relative to the *total* variation in all OECD countries, which is set at 100.

Substantial variation between schools and less variation among students within schools (*e.g.* in Hungary and Poland) indicates that students are generally in schools where other students perform at levels similar to their own. This selectivity may reflect family choice of school or residential location, policies on school enrolment, or allocation of students. On average across OECD countries, 36% of the total variation in student performance in reading literacy is attributable to variation between schools.

In Austria, Belgium, the Czech Republic, Germany, Greece, Hungary, Italy, Mexico and Poland, there is more variation between, than within, schools. In Korea, most of the variation is within schools but, more importantly, both within- and between-school variation are only around half of the OECD average. Korea thus not only achieves high average performance in reading and low overall disparity between students, but does so with relatively little variation in performance between schools. Spain also shows low overall variation (around three-quarters of the OECD average) and low between-school variation (16% of the OECD average for all variation) but, unlike Korea, has a mean score well below the OECD average. The smallest variation in reading performance between schools occurs in Finland, Iceland and Sweden, where it accounts for only between 7 and 11% of the average total student variation in OECD countries.

Overall, it is striking to see that in each of the seven countries with the highest mean scores in reading literacy (Australia, Canada, Finland, Ireland, Korea, New Zealand and the United Kingdom), differences between schools account for variations in performance that are less than a quarter of overall student variation in the average OECD country. These countries therefore succeed in securing high

average performance levels relatively consistently across schools. Conversely, there is a clear tendency for larger disparities among schools to be associated with lower overall performance.[16] This suggests that securing similar performance standards among schools, perhaps most importantly through identifying and reforming poorly performing schools, is not just an important policy goal in itself, but that it may also contribute to high overall performance.

4.4 Mitigating the impact of family background

The proportion of the variation in student performance within and between schools that is attributable to students' family background is also indicated in Figure 2.5. For example, in Sweden 17% of the within-school variation, and 73% of the between-school variation, is attributable to the family background factors measured by PISA. These percentages differ markedly from, say, those of Poland, where students' family background accounts for 2% of the within-school variation, and 10% of the between-school variation.

In comparing the extent to which the between-school differences are attributable to students' family backgrounds, it is important to take account of the size of the differences between schools. For example, family background factors account for more of the between-school differences in Sweden than in any other country, but Sweden (9%) has less variation in performance between schools than all other countries except Iceland (7%). Family background factors account for less of the between-school variation in Poland (10%) than in any other country, but Poland has more variation in performance between schools than in all but four other countries (Austria, Belgium, Germany and Hungary). In general, the greater the differences between schools, the smaller the proportion that can be attributed to students' family backgrounds.

Individual and school-level effects of family background

The analysis shows that, in many countries, a substantial portion of the between-school variation in performance in reading literacy is

---

16. The cross-country correlation between average performance and the proportion of the OECD average variation in student performance that is accounted for by schools is -.46.

Figure 2.6 Effects of student socio-economic background and school socio-economic composition on performance on the reading literacy scale, OECD countries, PISA 2000

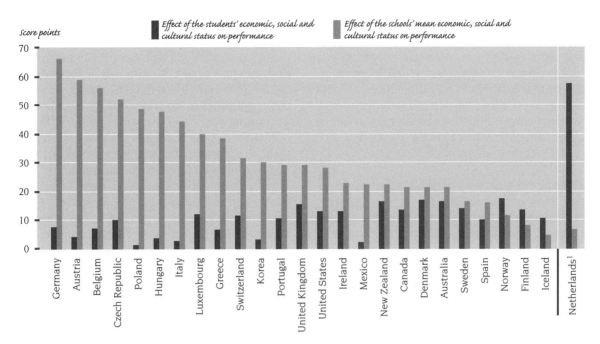

Note: The two columns for each country show the number of reading score points associated with an increase of half a standard deviation in (a) the measure of individual student economic, social and cultural status, and (b) the schools' mean economic, social and cultural status. These were estimated using a multi-level model that included gender, ethnicity, and student and school-level measures of family background ("economic, social and cultural status").

1. Response rate is too low to ensure comparability.

Source: OECD PISA database at *www.pisa.oecd.org*

Data for Figure 2.6, p. 63.

associated with differences in students' socio-economic backgrounds. This effect can operate in two ways. First, students' individual backgrounds may influence their performance. But in addition, the aggregate impact of the backgrounds of all the students enrolled in a school can also influence individual students. Understanding this collective impact is of key importance for policymakers wishing to provide all students with equal opportunities.

Schools whose intakes have a higher average level of socio-economic status tend to have several advantages. They are likely to have greater support from parents, fewer disciplinary problems, better qualified teachers and higher teacher morale, better teacher-student relations, and generally a school climate that is oriented towards higher performance. There is often also a faster-paced curriculum in such schools. Some of the "contextual effect" associated with high socio-

economic status may also stem from peer interactions as talented students work with each other. Peer pressure, peer competition and the focus in some schools on entry into tertiary education may also play a role.

Figure 2.6 estimates the strength of the relationship between reading literacy performance and socio-economic status, on the one hand of the individual student and on the other of all the students at a given school.[17] The lengths of the bars indicate the differences in scores in reading literacy associated with a given difference in the socio-economic status of different students,

---

17. These were estimated with a multilevel model (*i.e.* one that looks successively at the additional effect of a range of factors), taking account of economic, social and cultural status, gender, ethnicity, and family structure at the student level, and mean economic, social and cultural stuatus at the school level.

and the average socio-economic status of those enrolled in schools.[18]

In almost all countries there appears to be a clear advantage in attending a school whose students are, on average, from more advantaged family backgrounds. On average across OECD countries, this contextual effect is over three times as large as the direct effect associated with individual student background.[19] The socio-economic intake of the school thus has a strong association with student reading performance.[20]

Some of the observed contextual effect might be due to aspects of school quality. For example, to the extent that schools differentiated by academic tracking are also differentiated by socio-economic status, the school-level effect of socio-economic status would be reinforced by systematic curriculum differences. Some of the contextual effect might also be due to peer effects. But some of it might be due to other factors which are not accounted for in PISA, such as parental attitudes. Also, in many education systems students are allocated to different types of school or programme on the basis of factors which include their academic ability. Therefore, the findings should not lead to the conclusion that transferring a group of students from a school with a low socio-economic intake to a school with a high socio-economic intake would result automatically in the gains suggested by Figure 2.6.

Analysing the processes at work

In order to develop education policy in the light of these findings, there needs to be an understanding of the nature of the formal and informal mechanisms that contribute to between-school socio-economic differentiation, and its effect on students' performance. In some countries, students are highly differentiated along socio-economic lines, in part because of residential location and economic factors, but also because of features of the education system. Education policy in such countries might attempt to moderate the impact of socio-economic background on student performance by reducing the extent of differentiation along socio-economic lines, or by allocating resources to schools differentially. In these countries, it may be necessary to examine

how the allocation of school resources relates to the socio-economic intake of schools.

In other countries, structural features of the education system stream or track students into programmes with different curricula and teaching practices (this aspect is examined in more detail below). To the extent that the allocation of students to programmes in such systems is inter-linked with students' socio-economic background, those from disadvantaged backgrounds may not achieve their full potential. And in other countries, there is relatively little socio-economic differentiation, *i.e.*, schools tend to be similar in their socio-economic intake. Education policy in these countries might aim at moderating the impact of socio-economic background through measures aimed at improving school resources and reducing within-school differentiation according to students' economic, social and cultural status.

Table 2.4 shows that the combined influence of school-level factors, including those examined in the preceding section, explains about 31% of the variation between schools within countries, and 21% of the variation between countries. Students' individual family backgrounds, together with the mean socio-economic status of the school, explain

---

18. The score difference shown is for half a standard deviation of difference on the PISA index of economic, cultural and social status. What is important here is not the absolute value of these differences, but the comparison between individual student and whole-school effects across different countries.

19. A measure of 0.5 of a student-level standard deviation was chosen for the comparisons because this value describes realistic differences between schools in terms of their socio-economic composition. On average across OECD countries, the difference between the 75th and 25th quartiles of the school mean index of economic, social and cultural status is 0.72 of a student-level standard deviation and, in all but one OECD country, this difference is greater than, or equal to, half a student-level standard deviation on the socio-economic index.

20. Since no data on students' earlier achievement are available from PISA, it is not possible to determine to what extent the school background relates directly or indirectly to students' performance – by way of selection or self-selection, for example. In the interpretation of these findings, it also needs to be borne in mind that differences in the averages of schools' socio-economic backgrounds are naturally much smaller than comparable differences between individual students, given that every school's intake is mixed in terms of socio-economic variables.

about 12% of the differences between students within schools. On the other hand, they account for 66% of the differences in performance between schools and for 34% of the performance differences between countries. Together, family background and school factors explain most differences in performance between schools. On average, 72% of observed variation between schools within countries is accounted for by the combination of the school-level and student background factors identified through PISA.

The combined influence of school and background factors on differences in school performance is not simply the sum of the influence of school factors and that of background factors. This is because many characteristics of schools are closely associated with the characteristics of the families of their students. This means that some of the effect of family background on school results is *mediated* by the school characteristics.

Consider, for example, the predicted difference between PISA 2000 reading literacy scores in two schools whose students have different backgrounds – with a gap of one unit in their average scores on the index of economic, social and cultural status. In total, students at the school with students from higher-status backgrounds are expected to score 68 points more, on average, across OECD countries (see Table 2.4). Some of this difference arises because, on average, better-off students attend schools with features associated with better performance – this is the mediated portion. It accounts for about 11 of the 68 points in difference. The 11-point difference can be taken as an indicator of the extent to which school systems tend, on average, to reinforce the advantage of those students who already come from advantaged backgrounds. The remaining effect of student background – that which is not associated with school variables – accounts for 57 points.

Table 2.4 Effects of student-level and school-level factors on performance on the PISA reading literacy scale, for all OECD countries combined				
		Reading literacy scale		
	Increase	Model 1: impact of school factors[1]	Model 2: impact of family background[1]	Model 3: joint impact of school factors and family background[1]
		Effect S.E.	Effect S.E.	Effect S.E.
Family background and student characteristics				
Student-level index of economic, social and cultural status	1 unit		**20.1** (2.07)	**20.1** (2.07)
Student-level index of economic, social and cultural status squared			**-1.7** (0.34)	**-1.7** (0.35)
	1 student-level unit		**67.5** (6.48)	**56.6** (5.41)
Student is female			**25.5** (1.97)	**25.0** (2.03)
Student is foreign-born			**-23.2** (2.87)	**-23.1** (2.88)
Percentage of variance explained				
Students within schools		**0.0**	**12.4**	**12.4**
Schools within countries		**31.0**	**66.1**	**71.9**
Between countries		**20.8**	**34.3**	**43.4**

1. For an explanation of the models, see OECD (2001*a*).

* These indices were standardised to have a mean of 0 and a standard deviation of 1 for schools in OECD countries.

Effects marked in bold are statistically significant.

Source: OECD PISA database at *www.pisa.oecd.org* ....

It is possible to examine the extent to which the association between individual school factors (such as more resources) and higher performance can be accounted for by the more advantaged background of students who attend schools with better features. In most cases, the separate impact of the school factors becomes smaller once family background is taken into account, because many of the factors related to school quality are correlated with the school's economic, social and cultural status. For example, on average across OECD countries, PISA 2000 shows that half the reported effect of differences in school resources, and two-thirds of the effect of school size and student-teaching staff ratios, are associated with family background. In the case of variables describing school policy and practice, there is an even greater association. On the other hand, most of the impact of teacher-student relations and disciplinary climate is independent of family background.

Furthermore, beneficial school effects appear to be reinforced by socio-economic background. Schools with more resources and policies and practices associated with better student performance tend to have more advantaged students. For example, in Belgium, Germany and Luxembourg, larger numbers of specialist teachers[21] tend to be employed in schools with a more advantaged socio-economic background. Student responses generally indicate that schools with a higher socio-economic intake also have a better disciplinary climate. And finally, students in schools with high socio-economic status tend to use school resources more regularly than students in other schools (OECD, 2001a).

The overall conclusion is that the student's own home background is only part of the story of socio-economic disparities in education – and in most countries the smaller part. The net result is that in countries where there is a high degree of differentiation between schools along socio-economic lines, students from disadvantaged socio-economic backgrounds do worse. This, in turn, means that some of the *inequality of outcomes* is associated with *inequality of opportunity*. In such circumstances, talent remains unused and human resources are wasted. To the extent that the allocation of students to programmes in such systems is inter-linked with students' socio-economic background, those from disadvantaged backgrounds may not achieve their full potential.

4.5 Containing the impact of institutional differentiation

A much debated policy question is to what extent structural characteristics of educational systems moderate, or perhaps reinforce, socio-economic disparities. Table 2.5 displays some features of school systems that are relevant in this context.

One device to differentiate among students is the use of different institutions or programmes that seek to group students by their level of performance. Students of similar performance levels are sorted into the same type of institution or programme on the assumption that their talents will develop best in a learning environment in which they can stimulate each other equally well, and that an intellectually homogeneous student body will be conducive to the efficiency of teaching. The measure shown in Table 2.5 range from essentially undivided secondary education until age 15 to systems with four school types or distinct educational programmes (Austria, Hungary, the Netherlands and Switzerland). A specific aspect of such differentiation is the separate provision of general academic and vocational programmes. Vocational programmes differ from academic ones not only with regard to their curriculum, but also in that they generally prepare students for specific types of occupations and, in some cases, for direct entry into the labour market.

Another important dimension is the age at which decisions between different school types are generally made, and therefore students and their parents are faced with choices. Such decisions occur very early in Austria and Germany, at around age 10. By contrast, in countries such as New Zealand, Spain and the United States no formal differentiation takes place until the completion of secondary education.[22] Grade repetition can

---

21. For the purpose of this analysis, specialist teachers are defined as teachers with a university-level qualification with a major in the subject area assessed by PISA.

22. Since PISA assessed 15-year-olds, it only allows inferences concerning stratification introduced prior to that age. There is a clear tendency for overall variation in student performance and the impact of socio-economic background on performance to be greater the earlier institutional stratification starts. The association is strongest in countries that begin institutional stratification in the age range 10-12 years.

	First age of selection in the education system[1]	Variation in grade levels in which 15-year-olds are enrolled[2]	Number of school types or distinct educational programmes available to 15-year-olds	Proportion of 15-year-olds enrolled in pre-vocational educational programmes[1]	Total variation in student performance between schools
Australia	a	0.47	a	23	21
Austria	10	0.61	4	44	69
Belgium (Fl.)	12	0.59	3	18	76
Belgium (Fr.)	12	0.59	4	18	76
Canada	a	0.48	a	22	17
Czech Republic	11	0.55	4	16	52
Denmark	16	0.28	a	0	20
Finland	16	0.32	a	0	11
France	15	0.69	3	9	m
Germany	10	0.63	3	30	75
Greece	15	0.46	2	27	54
Hungary	11	0.59	4	30	71
Iceland	16	0.00	a	0	7
Ireland	15	0.84	3	2	17
Italy	14	0.52	3	0	51
Japan	15	0.00	3	26	37
Korea	14	0.13	2	35	20
Luxembourg	13	0.70	3	18	33
Mexico	12	0.79	4	40	43
Netherlands	12	0.60	5	20	m
New Zealand	a	0.35	a	0	20
Norway	16	0.11	a	m	13
Poland	15	m	3	27	67
Portugal	15	0.95	2	5	38
Spain	16	0.50	a	0	16
Sweden	16	0.15	a	0	9
Switzerland	15	0.50	4	2	49
United Kingdom	a	0.50	a	5	22
United States	a	0.55	a	0	35

Table 2.5 Structural features of school systems

a: not applicable.

m: missing data.

1. Pre-vocational programmes are defined as education mainly designed as an introduction to the world of work and as preparation for further vocational or technical education. Different from vocational programmes, pre-vocational programmes do not lead to a labour-market relevant qualification.

2. As measured by the standard deviation of grade levels among the 15-year-old students that were assessed by PISA.

Source: OECD PISA database at *www.pisa.oecd.org*; OECD (1999); OECD (2001*b*).

also be considered as a form of differentiation in that it seeks to adapt curriculum content to student performance.[23]

It is difficult to define these measures of differentiation in ways that are cross-nationally comparable and interpretable. However, the analysis shows that these indicators are highly interrelated so that it is possible to combine them into an index of educational institutional differentiation.[24] This index can then be related to the impact that the social background of students has on student performance. This analysis shows that the total effect of differentiation on the relationship between

social background and student reading performance is 0.55, as measured by the standardised regression coefficient. The extent of institutional differentiation is thus a strong predictor of the impact that family background has on student performance.

---

23. In PISA, grade repetition was estimated indirectly by calculating the standard deviation in the grade levels reported by students for each of the countries. Note that this measure also captures the degree to which students enter school earlier or later than the statutory entry age and may therefore overstate apparent grade repetition.

24. For the purpose of this analysis, the normalised components were added with equal weight.

The more differentiated and selective an education system is, the larger are the typical performance differences between students from more and less advantaged family backgrounds. This is true for the various aspects of family background that were measured by PISA, and it remains true even when control variables such as national income are taken into account. As a result, both overall variation in student performance and performance differences between schools tend to be greater in those countries with explicit differentiation between types of programme and schools at an early age.

The question remains whether differentiation might still contribute to raising overall performance levels. This question cannot be answered conclusively with a cross-sectional survey such as PISA. However, it is striking that the three best performing countries – Finland, Japan and Korea – show a very moderate degree of institutional differentiation combined with a consistently high level of student performance across schools and among students from different family backgrounds. By contrast, among the countries with a high degree of institutional differentiation, only Austria and the Flemish Community of Belgium perform significantly above the OECD average.

An explanation for these results is not straightforward. There is no intrinsic reason why institutional differentiation should necessarily lead to greater variation in student performance, or even to greater social selectivity. If teaching homogeneous groups of students is more efficient than teaching heterogeneous groups, this should increase the overall level of student performance rather than the dispersion of scores. However, in homogeneous environments, while the high performing students may profit from the wider opportunities to learn from one another, and stimulate each other's performance, the low performers may not be able to access effective models and support. It may also be that in highly differentiated systems it is easier to move students not meeting certain performance standards to other schools, tracks or streams with lower performance expectations, rather than investing the effort to raise their performance. Finally, it could be that a learning environment that has a greater variety of student abilities and backgrounds may stimulate teachers to use approaches that involve a higher degree of individual attention for students.

It is difficult to discern conclusive evidence for these possible explanations from PISA. However, it is noteworthy that the majority of the countries in which students report a comparatively low level of individual support from their teachers are also those with a particularly high degree of institutional differentiation.[25]

These arguments alone still do not explain the greater social selectivity of differentiated school systems that PISA 2000 demonstrates. Even if institutional differentiation leads to more variation in student performance, it does not necessarily increase the gap in performance between students from advantaged and disadvantaged backgrounds. One possible explanation is that more homogeneous learning environments for low performing students decrease the aspirations of parents and children from lower socio-economic backgrounds, and increase the aspirations of families from higher socio-economic backgrounds. In other words, the very existence of a highly differentiated system may signal to students and parents from lower socio-economic backgrounds what to expect from school.

The reason why the age at which differentiation begins is closely associated with social selectivity may be easier to explain. Students are more dependent upon their parents and their parental resources when they are younger and, in systems with a high degree of educational differentiation, parents from higher socio-economic backgrounds are in a better position to promote their children's chances than in a system in which such decisions are taken at a later age, and students themselves play a bigger role.

5. CONCLUSION

The PISA 2000 assessments of performance by 15-year-olds revealed wide differences among countries, and between schools and students within countries. Countries varied both in their average performance,

---

25. In the Czech Republic, Germany, Italy and Luxembourg, for example, at least 51% of students say that their teachers of the language of assessment never show interest in every student's learning or do so only in some lessons (as opposed to most lessons or every lesson), at least 27% of students say that their teachers never or only in some lessons provide an opportunity for students to express their opinions, and 58% or more of students say that their teachers never or only in some lessons help them with their learning. For a further analysis of the relationship between teacher support and student performance, see OECD (2001a).

and in the extent of spread around the average. They also differed in the extent to which family background shaped student performance.

A number of countries managed to combine high levels of performance with a relatively narrow range of differences among students. The performance of such countries provides considerable grounds for optimism. The results achieved by students in countries such as Finland, Canada, Korea and Japan indicate that it is possible to combine high performance standards with an equitable distribution of learning outcomes. Quality and equity do not have to be seen as competing policy objectives.

However, even the countries that performed well overall in the 2000 PISA assessments have areas for concern. In almost all countries there is a significant minority of students who performed at reading literacy Level 1 or below. Such students may struggle not just in school, but will find it difficult to make their way successfully in the world beyond school. In no single country does students' home background fail to have an influence on their school performance, but in some countries this influence is much less marked than in others.

A study such as PISA cannot, on its own, provide clear-cut answers on the factors that explain different levels of student, school and national performance, or the strategies that countries should use. However, one of the great advantages of cross-national studies is that they can show countries their areas of relative strength and weakness, and stimulate debate about current policies and practices.

In seeking to lift overall performance, and to reduce the impact of socio-economic background,

the PISA results provide a number of policy pointers. Important among these are building students' engagement with reading and school more generally, focusing on learning outcomes rather than educational inputs, providing schools with the authority for organising their own programmes – and holding them accountable for the results – and reducing the extent of social and educational differentiation among schools.

The PISA results also pose important questions for deeper investigation. For example, the strength of the findings on student engagement challenge school systems and researchers to delve more deeply into the motivational factors that make learning more effective – and how those factors can be developed. The strong association between student performance and structural differentiation in schooling challenges systems that stream students from a relatively early age to better understand the social and educational processes that are at work.

Such issues will be pursued in many different ways in the context of each country. But in addition, PISA itself is an ongoing process that aims progressively to develop a richer knowledge base with greater explanatory value. Future developments in PISA will help to deepen our understanding of the ways in which system policies and school practices affect the performance of students from different social backgrounds. The PISA assessments are being administered in 12 more non-OECD countries during 2002, and in 2003 the second full round of assessments will be conducted with an expanded range of learning areas. At both international and national levels research studies are underway to add further to the knowledge base in this area of prime policy importance.

References

OECD (1999), *Classifying Educational Programmes. Manual for the ISCED-97 Implementation in OECD Countries*, Paris.

OECD (2001*a*), *Knowledge and Skills for Life – First Results from* PISA 2000, Paris.

OECD (2001*b*), *Education at a Glance – OECD Indicators*, Paris.

OECD (2002*a*), PISA 2000 *Technical Report*, Paris.

OECD (2002*b*), *Education at a Glance – OECD Indicators* 2002, Paris.

Data for Figure 2.1

Percentage of students performing at each proficiency level on the PISA reading literacy scale, PISA 2000

	PISA reading literacy proficiency levels											
	Below Level 1 (less than 335 score points)		Level 1 (from 335 to 407 score points)		Level 2 (from 408 to 480 score points)		Level 3 (from 481 to 552 score points)		Level 4 (from 553 to 625 score points)		Level 5 (above 625 score points)	
	Percentage	S.E.	Percentage	S.E.	Percentage	S.E.	Percentage	S.E.	Percentage	S.E.	Percentage	S.E.
Australia	3.3	(0.5)	9.1	(0.8)	19.0	(1.1)	25.7	(1.1)	25.3	(0.9)	17.6	(1.2)
Austria	4.4	(0.4)	10.2	(0.6)	21.7	(0.9)	29.9	(1.2)	24.9	(1.0)	8.8	(0.8)
Belgium	7.7	(1.0)	11.3	(0.7)	16.8	(0.7)	25.8	(0.9)	26.3	(0.9)	12.0	(0.7)
Canada	2.4	(0.3)	7.2	(0.3)	18.0	(0.4)	28.0	(0.5)	27.7	(0.6)	16.8	(0.5)
Czech Republic	6.1	(0.6)	11.4	(0.7)	24.8	(1.2)	30.9	(1.1)	19.8	(0.8)	7.0	(0.6)
Denmark	5.9	(0.6)	12.0	(0.7)	22.5	(0.9)	29.5	(1.0)	22.0	(0.9)	8.1	(0.5)
Finland	1.7	(0.5)	5.2	(0.4)	14.3	(0.7)	28.7	(0.8)	31.6	(0.9)	18.5	(0.9)
France	4.2	(0.6)	11.0	(0.8)	22.0	(0.8)	30.6	(1.0)	23.7	(0.9)	8.5	(0.6)
Germany	9.9	(0.7)	12.7	(0.6)	22.3	(0.8)	26.8	(1.0)	19.4	(1.0)	8.8	(0.5)
Greece	8.7	(1.2)	15.7	(1.4)	25.9	(1.4)	28.1	(1.7)	16.7	(1.4)	5.0	(0.7)
Hungary	6.9	(0.7)	15.8	(1.2)	25.0	(1.1)	28.8	(1.3)	18.5	(1.1)	5.1	(0.8)
Iceland	4.0	(0.3)	10.5	(0.6)	22.0	(0.8)	30.8	(0.9)	23.6	(1.1)	9.1	(0.7)
Ireland	3.1	(0.5)	7.9	(0.8)	17.9	(0.9)	29.7	(1.1)	27.1	(1.1)	14.2	(0.8)
Italy	5.4	(0.9)	13.5	(0.9)	25.6	(1.0)	30.6	(1.0)	19.5	(1.1)	5.3	(0.5)
Japan	2.7	(0.6)	7.3	(1.1)	18.0	(1.3)	33.3	(1.3)	28.8	(1.7)	9.9	(1.1)
Korea	0.9	(0.2)	4.8	(0.6)	18.6	(0.9)	38.8	(1.1)	31.1	(1.2)	5.7	(0.6)
Luxembourg	14.2	(0.7)	20.9	(0.8)	27.5	(1.3)	24.6	(1.1)	11.2	(0.5)	1.7	(0.3)
Mexico	16.1	(1.2)	28.1	(1.4)	30.3	(1.1)	18.8	(1.2)	6.0	(0.7)	0.9	(0.2)
New Zealand	4.8	(0.5)	8.9	(0.5)	17.2	(0.9)	24.6	(1.1)	25.8	(1.1)	18.7	(1.0)
Norway	6.3	(0.6)	11.2	(0.8)	19.5	(0.8)	28.1	(0.8)	23.7	(0.9)	11.2	(0.7)
Poland	8.7	(1.0)	14.6	(1.0)	24.1	(1.4)	28.2	(1.3)	18.6	(1.3)	5.9	(1.0)
Portugal	9.6	(1.0)	16.7	(1.2)	25.3	(1.0)	27.5	(1.2)	16.8	(1.1)	4.2	(0.5)
Spain	4.1	(0.5)	12.2	(0.9)	25.7	(0.7)	32.8	(1.0)	21.1	(0.9)	4.2	(0.5)
Sweden	3.3	(0.4)	9.3	(0.6)	20.3	(0.7)	30.4	(1.0)	25.6	(1.0)	11.2	(0.7)
Switzerland	7.0	(0.7)	13.3	(0.9)	21.4	(1.0)	28.0	(1.0)	21.0	(1.0)	9.2	(1.0)
United Kingdom	3.6	(0.4)	9.2	(0.5)	19.6	(0.7)	27.5	(0.9)	24.4	(0.9)	15.6	(1.0)
United States	6.4	(1.2)	11.5	(1.2)	21.0	(1.2)	27.4	(1.3)	21.5	(1.4)	12.2	(1.4)
OECD average	**6.0**	**(0.1)**	**11.9**	**(0.2)**	**21.7**	**(0.2)**	**28.7**	**(0.2)**	**22.3**	**(0.2)**	**9.5**	**(0.1)**
Non-OECD countries												
Brazil	23.3	(1.4)	32.5	(1.2)	27.7	(1.3)	12.9	(1.1)	3.1	(0.5)	0.6	(0.2)
Latvia	12.7	(1.3)	17.9	(1.3)	26.3	(1.1)	25.2	(1.3)	13.8	(1.1)	4.1	(0.6)
Liechtenstein	7.6	(1.5)	14.5	(2.1)	23.2	(2.9)	30.1	(3.4)	19.5	(2.2)	5.1	(1.6)
Russian Federation	9.0	(1.0)	18.5	(1.1)	29.2	(0.8)	26.9	(1.1)	13.3	(1.0)	3.2	(0.5)

Data for the Netherlands were not included because the response rate was too low to ensure comparability.
Source: OECD PISA database at *www.pisa.oecd.org*

Education Policy Analysis

Data for Figure 2.2

Student performance on the PISA reading literacy scale and expenditure per student, OECD countries

	Performance on the reading literacy scale		Cumulative expenditure on educational institutions per student from 6 to 15 years of age (US dollars[1]) (1998)
	Mean score	S.E.	
Australia	528	(3.5)	44 623
Austria	507	(2.4)	71 387
Belgium	507	(3.6)	46 338
Czech Republic	492	(2.4)	21 384
Denmark	497	(2.4)	65 794
Finland	546	(2.6)	45 363
France	505	(2.7)	50 481
Germany	484	(2.5)	41 978
Greece	474	(5.0)	27 356
Hungary	480	(4.0)	20 277
Ireland	527	(3.2)	31 015
Italy	487	(2.9)	60 824
Japan	522	(5.2)	53 255
Korea	525	(2.4)	30 844
Mexico	422	(3.3)	11 239
Norway	505	(2.8)	61 677
Poland	479	(4.5)	16 154
Portugal	470	(4.5)	36 521
Spain	493	(2.7)	36 699
Sweden	516	(2.2)	53 386
Switzerland	494	(4.3)	64 266
United Kingdom	523	(2.6)	42 793
United States	504	(7.1)	67 313

1. US dollars converted using PPPs.
Source: OECD PISA database at *www.pisa.oecd.org*; OECD (2001*b*).

Data for Figure 2.3

Performance in reading and the impact of family background, OECD countries, PISA 2000

	Performance on the PISA reading literacy scale[2]				Mean PISA socio-economic index of occupational status[1]				Score point difference associated with one unit on the index of ESCS[1, 2, 3]		Difference between 95th and 5th percentiles of the student distribution on the index of ESCS[3]
	Mean score	S.E.	Standard deviation	S.E.	Bottom quarter	S.E.	Top quarter	S.E.	Difference	S.E.	
Australia	**528**	(3.5)	102	(1.6)	31.1	(0.2)	73.2	(0.3)	**46**	(2.36)	2.9
Austria	**507**	(2.4)	93	(1.6)	32.9	(0.2)	69.1	(0.3)	41	(2.26)	2.7
Belgium	**507**	(3.6)	107	(2.4)	28.4	(0.1)	71.8	(0.2)	**48**	(2.35)	3.1
Canada	**534**	(1.6)	95	(1.1)	31.3	(0.1)	72.9	(0.1)	**37**	(1.31)	2.8
Czech Republic	**492**	(2.4)	96	(1.9)	31.2	(0.2)	66.1	(0.3)	**50**	(2.22)	2.7
Denmark	497	(2.4)	98	(1.8)	29.0	(0.2)	71.1	(0.3)	42	(2.07)	2.8
Finland	**546**	(2.6)	89	(2.6)	29.7	(0.2)	71.8	(0.2)	**30**	(2.40)	2.9
France	505	(2.7)	92	(1.7)	27.7	(0.2)	71.2	(0.3)	47	(2.17)	2.9
Germany	**484**	(2.5)	111	(1.9)	30.0	(0.2)	70.2	(0.2)	**60**	(3.44)	2.8
Greece	**474**	(5.0)	97	(2.7)	25.6	(0.3)	72.3	(0.4)	38	(3.05)	3.3
Hungary	**480**	(4.0)	94	(2.1)	30.4	(0.2)	71.5	(0.2)	**53**	(2.89)	2.9
Iceland	**507**	(1.5)	92	(1.4)	31.4	(0.2)	73.8	(0.2)	**24**	(2.05)	2.8
Ireland	**527**	(3.2)	94	(1.7)	28.5	(0.2)	69.4	(0.2)	38	(2.22)	2.9
Italy	**487**	(2.9)	91	(2.7)	28.5	(0.1)	68.9	(0.4)	32	(2.35)	3.1
Japan	**522**	(5.2)	86	(3.0)	m	m	m	m	21	(2.87)	2.6
Korea	**525**	(2.4)	70	(1.6)	26.5	(0.1)	62.9	(0.5)	21	(2.37)	2.9
Luxembourg	**441**	(1.6)	100	(1.5)	25.1	(0.1)	66.1	(0.4)	46	(1.69)	3.4
Mexico	**422**	(3.3)	86	(2.1)	24.4	(0.1)	66.5	(0.5)	35	(2.47)	4.4
New Zealand	**529**	(2.8)	108	(2.0)	30.5	(0.3)	73.6	(0.2)	45	(2.27)	3.1
Norway	505	(2.8)	104	(1.7)	35.6	(0.2)	73.9	(0.2)	41	(1.83)	2.9
Poland	**479**	(4.5)	100	(3.1)	27.3	(0.2)	67.0	(0.4)	36	(3.40)	3.2
Portugal	**470**	(4.5)	97	(1.8)	26.8	(0.2)	65.7	(0.5)	40	(2.09)	3.6
Spain	**493**	(2.7)	85	(1.2)	26.8	(0.1)	67.3	(0.5)	32	(1.52)	3.3
Sweden	**516**	(2.2)	92	(1.2)	30.4	(0.2)	72.1	(0.2)	**36**	(1.86)	2.7
Switzerland	494	(4.3)	102	(2.0)	29.3	(0.2)	71.9	(0.3)	**49**	(2.24)	3.0
United Kingdom	**523**	(2.6)	100	(1.5)	30.7	(0.2)	71.8	(0.2)	**49**	(1.87)	2.9
United States	504	(7.1)	105	(2.7)	30.3	(0.2)	72.5	(0.3)	**48**	(2.75)	3.3
OECD average	**500**	**(0.6)**	**100**	**(0.4)**	**29.3**	**(0.0)**	**70.2**	**(0.1)**	**41**	**(0.97)**	**3.0**

m: missing data.

1. For the definition of these indices, see OECD (2001*a*).
2. Values marked in bold are statistically significantly different from the OECD average.
3. ESCS: economic, social and cultural status.

Source: OECD PISA database at *www.pisa.oecd.org*; OECD (2001*a*).

IMPROVING BOTH QUALITY AND EQUITY:
INSIGHTS FROM PISA 2000

Data for Figure 2.4
Percentage of students enrolled in schools which have at least some responsibility for the following aspects of school policy and management, OECD countries, PISA 2000

Results based on reports from school principals and reported proportionate to the number of 15-year-olds enrolled in the school

	Performance on the PISA reading literacy scale		Appointing teachers		Dismissing teachers		Establishing teachers' starting salaries		Determining teachers' salary increases		Formulating the school budget	
	Mean score	S.E.	%	S.E.	%	S.E.	%	S.E.	%	S.E	%	S.E
Australia	528	(3.5)	60	(2.2)	47	(3.1)	18	(2.2)	19	(2.6)	96	(1.5)
Austria	507	(2.4)	15	(2.9)	5	(1.7)	1	(0.5)	1	(0.5)	14	(2.7)
Belgium	507	(3.6)	96	(1.3)	95	(1.4)	7	(1.7)	7	(1.8)	98	(1.0)
Canada	534	(1.6)	82	(1.2)	61	(1.7)	34	(1.8)	34	(1.7)	77	(1.4)
Czech Republic	492	(2.4)	96	(1.2)	95	(1.3)	70	(3.1)	73	(3.1)	83	(2.6)
Denmark	497	(2.4)	97	(1.3)	57	(3.2)	13	(2.5)	15	(2.7)	89	(2.2)
Finland	546	(2.6)	35	(3.8)	21	(3.3)	1	(0.8)	2	(1.0)	56	(3.9)
France	505	(2.7)	m	m	m	m	m	m	m	m	m	m
Germany	484	(2.5)	10	(2.3)	4	(1.3)	2	(0.9)	11	(2.2)	13	(2.0)
Greece	474	(5.0)	65	(4.7)	70	(4.4)	73	(4.3)	77	(3.9)	87	(3.4)
Hungary	480	(4.0)	100	(0.0)	99	(1.0)	41	(4.3)	50	(4.3)	61	(4.1)
Iceland	507	(1.5)	99	(0.0)	99	(0.1)	4	(0.1)	7	(0.1)	76	(0.2)
Ireland	527	(3.2)	88	(2.5)	73	(3.0)	4	(1.7)	5	(2.2)	79	(3.1)
Italy	487	(2.9)	10	(2.1)	11	(2.6)	1	(0.8)	1	(0.8)	94	(2.4)
Japan	522	(5.2)	33	(1.9)	32	(2.0)	32	(2.0)	32	(2.0)	50	(3.3)
Korea	525	(2.4)	32	(4.1)	22	(4.0)	15	(3.1)	7	(2.4)	88	(2.5)
Luxembourg	441	(1.6)	m	m	m	m	m	m	m	m	100	(0.0)
Mexico	422	(3.3)	57	(3.4)	48	(3.8)	26	(3.1)	28	(3.1)	68	(4.2)
New Zealand	529	(2.8)	100	(0.0)	99	(0.8)	17	(2.4)	41	(3.3)	98	(1.1)
Norway	505	(2.8)	m	m	m	m	m	m	m	m	m	m
Poland	479	(4.5)	m	m	m	m	m	m	m	m	m	m
Portugal	470	(4.5)	13	(2.1)	9	(1.2)	1	(0.7)	1	(0.7)	89	(2.9)
Spain	493	(2.7)	38	(2.5)	39	(2.6)	9	(2.2)	9	(2.2)	90	(2.5)
Sweden	516	(2.2)	99	(0.8)	83	(3.2)	62	(3.6)	74	(3.6)	85	(3.1)
Switzerland	494	(4.3)	93	(1.7)	82	(2.3)	13	(2.7)	15	(3.0)	54	(3.3)
United Kingdom	523	(2.6)	99	(0.3)	89	(1.3)	72	(3.0)	70	(3.1)	92	(0.8)
United States	504	(7.1)	97	(0.9)	98	(1.2)	76	(4.9)	74	(5.1)	96	(1.9)
OECD average	**500**	**(0.6)**	**61**	**(0.4)**	**54**	**(0.5)**	**23**	**(0.5)**	**26**	**(0.5)**	**76**	**(0.6)**
Cross-country correlation between country's average achievement on the reading literacy scale and the percentage of students[1]			0.16		0.10		-0.05		-0.06		0.00	
Netherlands[2]			100	(0.0)	100	(0.0)	71	(5.0)	45	(5.6)	100	(0.0)

m: missing data.

1. Correlation values indicated in bold are statistically significant.
2. Response rate is too low to ensure comparability.

Source: OECD PISA database at www.pisa.oecd.org; OECD (2001a).

Data for Figure 2.4 (*continued*)
Percentage of students enrolled in schools which have at least some responsibility for the following aspects of school policy and management, OECD countries, PISA 2000

Results based on reports from school principals and reported proportionate to the number of 15-year-olds enrolled in the school

	Deciding on budget allocations within the school		Establishing student disciplinary policies		Establishing student assessment policies		Approving students for admittance to school		Choosing which textbooks are used		Determining course content		Deciding which courses are offered	
	%	S.E.	%	S.E.	%	S.E.	%	S.E.	%	S.E.	%	S.E.	%	S.E.
Australia	100	(0.2)	100	(0.2)	99	(0.6)	94	(1.6)	100	(0.2)	84	(3.2)	96	(1.8)
Austria	93	(2.0)	96	(1.6)	69	(3.5)	75	(2.9)	99	(0.7)	54	(3.6)	57	(3.7)
Belgium	99	(0.6)	99	(0.9)	100	(0.4)	95	(1.7)	99	(0.6)	59	(3.7)	61	(3.6)
Canada	99	(0.3)	98	(0.5)	94	(1.0)	89	(1.0)	89	(0.9)	49	(1.8)	90	(1.1)
Czech Republic	99	(0.6)	100	(0.5)	100	(0.3)	89	(1.7)	100	(0.0)	82	(2.9)	82	(2.8)
Denmark	98	(1.0)	99	(0.8)	87	(2.4)	87	(2.6)	100	(0.0)	90	(1.9)	77	(2.6)
Finland	99	(0.9)	96	(1.9)	89	(2.6)	54	(4.0)	100	(0.0)	91	(2.3)	95	(2.0)
France	m	m	m	m	m	m	m	m	m	m	m	m	m	m
Germany	96	(1.3)	95	(1.4)	79	(2.8)	79	(3.0)	96	(1.7)	35	(3.3)	35	(3.4)
Greece	95	(2.1)	97	(1.5)	94	(2.2)	90	(2.5)	90	(2.9)	92	(2.6)	89	(2.9)
Hungary	92	(2.3)	100	(0.0)	98	(1.0)	99	(0.7)	100	(0.4)	97	(1.3)	98	(1.0)
Iceland	87	(0.1)	99	(0.0)	98	(0.1)	74	(0.1)	99	(0.0)	79	(0.2)	62	(0.2)
Ireland	100	(0.0)	99	(0.6)	99	(0.9)	95	(2.0)	100	(0.0)	37	(4.1)	97	(1.3)
Italy	57	(5.0)	100	(0.0)	100	(0.0)	63	(5.1)	100	(0.0)	93	(2.9)	22	(4.0)
Japan	91	(2.9)	100	(0.4)	100	(0.0)	100	(0.0)	99	(0.7)	99	(0.7)	98	(1.3)
Korea	95	(1.7)	100	(0.0)	99	(0.1)	97	(1.4)	99	(0.6)	99	(0.6)	93	(2.3)
Luxembourg	100	(0.0)	m	m	m	m	100	(0.0)	m	m	m	m	m	m
Mexico	77	(3.7)	99	(0.7)	92	(2.5)	86	(2.4)	81	(3.0)	59	(4.1)	58	(3.4)
New Zealand	100	(0.0)	100	(0.0)	100	(0.0)	94	(1.2)	100	(0.0)	87	(2.7)	100	(0.1)
Norway	m	m	m	m	m	m	m	m	m	m	m	m	m	m
Poland	m	m	m	m	m	m	m	m	m	m	m	m	m	m
Portugal	95	(2.0)	92	(2.2)	88	(2.6)	85	(3.1)	100	(0.0)	20	(3.4)	54	(4.5)
Spain	98	(1.3)	99	(0.8)	97	(1.5)	89	(2.4)	100	(0.4)	86	(2.9)	54	(3.8)
Sweden	99	(0.6)	100	(0.0)	97	(1.5)	54	(4.0)	100	(0.0)	88	(2.8)	76	(3.7)
Switzerland	87	(2.9)	98	(1.2)	75	(3.6)	82	(3.0)	51	(4.1)	29	(3.5)	34	(3.4)
United Kingdom	100	(0.1)	99	(0.5)	100	(0.2)	66	(3.6)	100	(0.0)	94	(1.5)	100	(0.1)
United States	99	(1.0)	99	(0.9)	93	(2.2)	89	(2.6)	92	(3.0)	84	(4.3)	97	(1.3)
OECD average	**94**	**(0.3)**	**95**	**(0.2)**	**89**	**(0.4)**	**84**	**(0.5)**	**92**	**(0.2)**	**69**	**(0.6)**	**71**	**(0.6)**
Cross-country correlation between country's average achievement on the reading literacy scale and the percentage of students[1]	**0.37**		0.21		0.20		-0.21		0.30		0.25		**0.51**	
Netherlands[2]	100	(0.0)	100	(0.0)	100	(0.0)	100	(0.0)	100	(0.0)	92	(3.2)	95	(2.4)

m: missing data.

1. Correlation values indicated in bold are statistically significant.
2. Response rate is too low to ensure comparability.

Source: OECD PISA database at *www.pisa.oecd.org*; OECD (2001a).

Data for Figure 2.5

Variations in reading literacy performance between and within schools, OECD countries, PISA 2000

	Total variation in student performance[1]	Variation expressed as a percentage of the average variation in student performance across the OECD countries			Percentage of between-school variance that is explained by socio-economic background factors	Percentage of within-school variance that is explained by socio-economic background factors
		Total variation in student performance expressed as a percentage of the average variation in student performance across OECD countries	Proportion of average variation in student performance that lies between schools	Proportion of average variation in student performance that lies within schools		
Australia	10 357	111.6	20.9	90.6	64	16
Austria	8 649	93.2	68.6	45.7	28	5
Belgium	11 455	123.5	76.0	50.9	31	9
Canada	8 955	96.5	17.1	80.1	42	14
Czech Republic	9 278	100.0	51.9	45.3	43	11
Denmark	9 614	103.6	19.6	85.9	58	18
Finland	7 994	86.2	10.7	76.5	18	20
France	m	m	m	m	m	m
Germany	12 368	133.3	74.8	50.2	27	12
Greece	9 436	101.7	53.8	52.9	25	8
Hungary	8 810	95.0	71.2	34.8	25	4
Iceland	8 529	91.9	7.0	85.0	31	12
Ireland	8 755	94.4	17.1	79.2	59	12
Italy	8 356	90.1	50.9	43.4	19	3
Japan[2]	7 358	79.3	36.5	43.9	11	3
Korea	4 833	52.1	19.7	33.0	17	3
Luxembourg	10 088	108.7	33.4	74.9	54	21
Mexico	7 370	79.4	42.9	37.4	31	4
New Zealand	11 701	126.1	20.1	103.9	70	19
Norway	10 743	115.8	12.6	102.4	48	20
Poland	9 958	107.3	67.0	38.9	10	2
Portugal	9 436	101.7	37.5	64.3	43	14
Spain	7 181	77.4	15.9	60.9	59	12
Sweden	8 495	91.6	8.9	83.0	73	17
Switzerland	10 408	112.2	48.7	63.7	35	18
United Kingdom	10 098	108.9	22.4	82.3	61	18
United States	10 979	118.3	35.1	83.6	61	17
OECD average	**9 277**	**100.0**	**36.2**	**65.1**	**34**	**14**

m: missing data.

1. The total variation in student performance is obtained as the square of the standard deviation shown in the data table for Figure 2.1. The statistical variance and not the standard deviation is used for this comparison to allow for the decomposition of the components of variation in student performance.

2. Due to the sampling methods used in Japan, the between-school variance in Japan includes variation between classes within schools.

Source: OECD PISA database at www.pisa.oecd.org; OECD (2001a).

Data for Figure 2.6
Effects of student socio-economic background and school socio-economic composition on performance on the reading literacy scale, OECD countries, PISA 2000

Effect of an increase of half a student-level standard deviation of the index of economic, social and cultural status[1]

	Interquartile range of school mean index of economic, social and cultural status	Effect of the students' economic, social and cultural status on performance	Effect of the schools' mean economic, social and cultural status on performance
Australia	0.73	17	21
Austria	0.83	4	59
Belgium	0.97	7	56
Canada	0.60	14	22
Czech Republic	0.52	10	52
Denmark	0.54	17	22
Finland	0.44	13	8
France	m	m	m
Germany	0.63	8	66
Greece	0.75	7	39
Hungary	0.86	4	47
Iceland	0.50	11	5
Ireland	0.55	13	23
Italy	1.04	3	44
Japan[2]	m	m	m
Korea	0.85	3	30
Luxembourg	0.96	12	40
Mexico	1.20	3	22
New Zealand	0.64	16	22
Norway	0.57	17	12
Poland	0.92	2	49
Portugal	0.66	11	29
Spain	0.77	10	16
Sweden	0.50	14	16
Switzerland	0.50	12	32
United Kingdom	0.93	15	29
United States	0.61	13	28
OECD average	**0.72**	**10**	**32**
Netherlands[3]	0.66	7	57

m: missing data.

1. The effects on reading performance were estimated using a multi-level model that included gender, ethnicity, and student and school-level measures of family background ("economic, social and cultural status").

2. Data for Japan are not included in this table due to a high percentage of missing data on parental education and parental occupation.

3. Response rate is too low to ensure comparability.

Source: OECD PISA database at *www.pisa.oecd.org*; OECD (2001a).

chapter 3
THE TEACHING WORKFORCE: CONCERNS AND POLICY CHALLENGES

▼

SUMMARY

There are serious concerns in many OECD countries about maintaining an adequate supply of good quality teachers. Teacher shortages may result not just in unfilled posts but in under-qualified staff or excessive teacher workloads. A teacher shortage raises quality as well as quantity concerns.

Defining and measuring shortfalls in teacher supply is not easy. However, there is clear evidence of difficulties faced by some countries. For example:

– In half of OECD countries, a majority of 15-year-olds attends schools whose principals think that student learning is hindered at least "a little" by a teacher shortage/ inadequacy.

– In certain countries, although by no means all, it is becoming harder to fill teaching posts.

– Attrition rates from the teacher profession vary widely across countries. In some, the majority of people leaving teaching are retiring; in others only a small minority.

– Teaching forces are ageing. In some OECD countries, over 40% of teachers are in their 50s.

– In almost all countries, teacher salaries fell relative to national income per head during the late 1990s.

Educational authorities in countries with the greatest difficulties face a combined challenge: to design incentives to attract high-quality candidates and former teachers to the pool of those who want to teach; exclude from the pool those who lack the skills to teach; and retain and further develop the skills of those effective teachers currently in the profession.

1. INTRODUCTION

The ability of schools to meet pressing needs depends critically on the teaching workforce. Yet there are serious concerns about the quality of teacher supply, and specifically about teacher shortages. OECD Education Ministers meeting in 2001 expressed their concerns as follows:

"Most of our countries face an ageing teaching force, a decline in the status of teaching and serious problems in recruitment. At the same time, there are demands on our institutions to teach in new ways and to fulfil new roles. [...] We have reviewed some of the future development options for our schools. The more optimistic of these could be jeopardised if a serious teacher shortage occurs. We need to explore together strategies to attract and retain high-quality teachers and school principals."

Such concerns are based on some disturbing signs of shortfalls in teacher supply. For example, in Australia, it has been estimated that the number of graduates qualifying as secondary teachers will meet only 70% of projected new demand by 2005 (Preston, 2000). In Canada, one in four teaching graduates do not become teachers, and an estimated 25-30% of those who start teaching leave within five years (Canadian Teachers' Federation, 2000). In Finland, it has been increasingly difficult to meet target enrolments in certain subject areas in teacher education programmes: in 1999 the shortfalls were 35% in mathematics and chemistry, 50% in computer science and 65% in physics (National Board of Education, Finland, 2000). The United States Department of Education estimates that 2.5 million additional teachers will be needed over the next decade, which is 200 000 more than at the present production rate of new teachers (Education Commission of the States, 2001).

The issues surrounding teacher shortages, and teacher quality more generally, are attracting much policy attention. A wide range of research studies has confirmed the importance of teacher quality for student learning (see Box 3.1). Teacher shortages and teacher quality are not necessarily

---

Box 3.1 The importance of teacher quality

A review of the literature indicates that a range of factors relating to teacher quality and teaching quality affects student performance (see OECD, 2001c). However, the literature also reveals the limitations of the information provided by the more measurable characteristics of teachers. Researchers have often found it hard to isolate the effect of characteristics such as subject-matter knowledge, qualifications, academic ability, pedagogical knowledge or teaching experience on student outcomes. The evidence predominantly shows a positive impact of these teacher characteristics on student learning, but to a lesser extent than may have been expected. A possible explanation is that research studies looking at individual school systems with relatively uniform teacher characteristics, are unable to observe sufficient variation in such factors to be able to measure the difference they make. In addition, for most of these characteristics, a "threshold effect" is likely to apply: teachers need a certain level of qualifications or experience to be effective, but further attainments beyond those levels may be progressively less important for student performance.

A further explanation is that the teacher characteristics that are typically measured in research studies might explain less of the variation in teacher quality than other characteristics that are more challenging to measure. These include the ability to convey ideas in clear and convincing ways; to work effectively with colleagues and the school community; to use a wide range of teaching strategies appropriate for student needs; and enthusiasm, creativity and commitment to students' success. The literature reviewed in OECD (2001c) includes recent studies that point to the importance of such variables in influencing student learning. Such results suggest that policy initiatives need to take account of the potentially substantial variation in quality that exists among teachers whose readily measured characteristics are similar.

associated: there can be quality concerns when no shortages are apparent, for example. However, where there are actual or looming teacher shortages, there must at least be a risk that teacher quality is reduced. In particular, where a school system *seeks* to recruit teachers with certain qualifications and experience, a failure to do so warns of a wider malaise that can damage teacher quality more widely than may be implied by lower competencies of teachers who lack the expected qualifications.

The analysis of teacher shortages is not straightforward. First, measuring the extent of a shortage is difficult, and no agreed measure presently exists at international level. This is partly because "teacher shortage" raises quality as well as quantity issues. School systems often respond to teacher shortages in the short term by some combination of: lowering qualification requirements for entry to the profession; assigning teachers to teach in subject areas in which they are not fully qualified; increasing the number of classes that teachers are allocated; or increasing class sizes. Such responses, which may mean that a shortage is not readily evident, nevertheless raise concerns about the quality of teaching and learning. In this chapter, *teacher shortage* is interpreted as a "lack of teachers meeting the qualification standards established by educational authorities". A *lack* of teachers means not enough to maintain teacher workloads and class sizes that are considered appropriate. In this definition, a shortage refers to a lack of *qualified* teachers. This concept is related, but not equivalent to, a lack of *quality* teachers. For example, if a country does not face a teacher shortage as defined above, it does not necessarily follow that the quality of the teaching workforce is adequate.

A second difficulty is the limited availability of international data on indicators that are closely associated with teacher shortages.[1] However, some individual countries have good, accessible data that provide useful insights on the recruitment and retention of qualified teachers. As a consequence, this chapter refers to some countries, especially the United Kingdom and the United States, more frequently than others. However, this does not mean that teacher issues are necessarily of greater concern in those countries that are cited most often.

This chapter is linked to the recently launched OECD activity *Attracting, Developing and Retaining Effective Teachers*, in which around 25 countries are taking part.[2] The chapter aims to summarise what is currently known about the nature and severity of teacher shortages among OECD countries. Section 2 characterises the shortage problem, and reviews the available evidence. Section 3 identifies the policy challenges that shortages give rise to, and outlines some policy tools. A summary and conclusions are provided in Section 4.

2. WHAT IS THE EVIDENCE ON TEACHER SHORTAGES?

The implications of teacher shortages can be analysed by looking at how educational systems respond to imbalances between demand for, and supply of, teachers. In the short-run, school systems facing situations of demand for teachers exceeding the available supply typically respond by:

– *Relaxing qualification requirements*. If a qualified applicant is not available to fill a teaching position, a less qualified applicant without full certification may be hired ("out-of-licence" teaching). Alternatively, teachers may be required to teach outside their areas of qualification: teachers trained in another field or level of schooling are assigned to teach in the understaffed area ("out-of-field" teaching). In addition, school systems may feel more pressure to retain poor performing teachers when teachers are generally in short supply.

– *Raising teaching loads*. The number of teachers required can be reduced and brought into line with the available supply by increasing the

---

1. The OECD is working with Member countries to improve the coverage and international comparability of data on teachers, including data on the teacher labour market.

2. The activity is intended to: (i) synthesise research on issues related to policies concerned with attracting, recruiting, retaining and developing effective teachers; (ii) identify innovative and successful policy initiatives and practices; (iii) facilitate exchanges of lessons and experiences among countries; and (iv) identify policy options. An important purpose is to identify data gaps concerning teachers and contribute to international efforts to improve data coverage and quality. The final report will be produced in 2004. Further information is available on *www.oecd.org/els/education/teacherpolicy*

workloads of teachers. This can be achieved by increasing class sizes and/or by increasing the average number of classes assigned to each teacher.

It is rarely the case that, when demand exceeds supply, a significant proportion of teaching positions remains unfilled. Hiring practices ensure that teachers are present to staff almost all classrooms. In this way, the immediate effect of a shortage is more likely to be a lower quality of teaching than a dramatic tale of classrooms full of students without teachers.

In the long-run, school systems have a wide range of strategies for enhancing the supply of teachers. The most commonly proposed response is to raise salaries to make the profession more competitive with other occupations. Additional strategies include improving working conditions, the status of the profession, and redesigning other incentives. These are described in more detail in Section 3.

2.1 Approaches to assessing teacher shortages

If teacher shortages rarely translate into empty classrooms, how can they be measured? A teacher shortage is a relative concept and depends on country-specific standards defining a "qualified" teacher. Thus, the meaning of a shortage is not necessarily the same across countries. It is not surprising, then, that there is no clear, universally agreed measure of what actually constitutes a teacher shortage.

Teacher shortages are generally indicated through two dimensions of the outcome of recruitment and assignment processes (Wilson and Pearson, 1993):

– *Vacancy rates*: The simplest measure is the *number of unfilled vacancies* for teachers. Despite its appeal, such a measure is not likely to be reliable on its own. All but a few vacancies can be filled in some way, whether through temporary or less qualified staff. Some schools might not create vacancies for staff if they are convinced that a particular post will not be filled by a teacher with the appropriate skills and abilities. However, even if a low proportion of unfilled vacancies does not necessarily mean the absence of shortages, a high level of unfilled vacancies provides evidence

of their presence. What is of greater interest is the *number of "difficult to fill" vacancies*, those that have been *"unfilled" for a significant period of time*, or the *proportion of positions filled by teachers without full certification status*.

– *"Hidden" shortages*: These are said to exist when teaching is carried out by someone who is not qualified to teach the subject. It is often referred to as "out-of-field" teaching and is usually measured as the *proportion of teachers teaching an area in which they are not qualified*. Nevertheless, this measure also suffers from certain limitations, as "out-of-field" teaching might result not only from shortages but also from the way schools are managed. In fact, many principals find that assigning teachers to teach out of their fields is often more convenient, less expensive or less time-consuming than the alternatives (Ingersoll, 1999).

These measures reveal, in a somewhat imperfect way, the extent to which school systems face problems in recruiting teachers. This problem is closely related to that of retaining teachers, as the demand for new teachers depends crucially on how many teachers leave the profession in a given year. For example, policies that improve salaries and other conditions for new recruits but which do not address the issues associated with teacher attrition may prove expensive and counter-productive. It is thus important to look also at the flows out of the teaching profession, through such indicators as *attrition rates, characteristics of leavers, or reasons for leaving the teaching profession*. The large size of the teaching force means that even a small rise of one or two percentage points in the attrition rate can have major consequences for the numbers of replacement teachers that need to be recruited.

Problems of teacher shortages are typically uneven. In some regions, subject areas, and educational levels, shortages can be particularly acute. For example, shortages tend to be more intense in subjects such as science and mathematics, in teaching fields such as special education, and in rural areas in some countries. Therefore, it is desirable to have disaggregated indicators that reflect these differences.

Information regarding the qualifications of the current stock of teachers is also important in

THE TEACHING WORKFORCE:
CONCERNS AND POLICY CHALLENGES

designing teacher policy. Useful information includes *the percentage of teachers holding a qualification in education, the distribution by highest qualification, certification status, years of experience, and level of participation in professional development activities.* Although such characteristics are only indirect and imperfect measures of quality, they do provide useful information on the teaching workforce.

Further, the *age distribution of the current teaching workforce* provides a basis for assessing how acute retirement-related supply shortages are likely to be. Also, evidence on factors related to the attractiveness of the profession, such as *relative salaries, fringe benefits and working conditions of teachers*, can prove useful in explaining the development of shortages. Finally, as an insufficient number of teachers is defined relative to given needs, it is also important to look at the pressures on the demand side, in particular at *expected changes in the size of the school-age population.*

2.2 Data on teacher shortages

This section uses a range of sources to provide data on the shortage indicators outlined in Section 2.1. It needs to be emphasised, though, that the indicators are imperfect measures, and the available evidence is far from complete in terms of the range of countries covered. To introduce the data, it is useful first to see what school principals think about the impact of teacher shortages on student learning.

School principals' perceptions

In 2000, secondary school principals in all but two OECD countries were asked whether, and to what extent, "the learning of 15-year-old students is hindered by a shortage/inadequacy of teachers". This question was part of the Programme for International Student Assessment (PISA) survey (OECD, 2001b). Figure 3.1 summarises the results.[3]

Figure 3.1 Principals' perceptions on whether a shortage/inadequacy of teachers hinders student learning, 2000

Percentage of 15-year-old students enrolled in schools where principals report that learning is hindered by a shortage/inadequacy of teachers to the following extent:

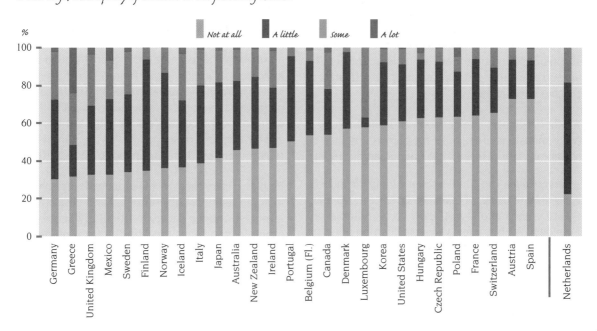

Note: For the Netherlands, the response rate is too low to ensure comparability.
Source: OECD PISA database at *www.pisa.oecd.org* ....
Data for Figure 3.1, p. 87.

Figure 3.2 Principals' perceptions on whether a shortage/inadequacy of teachers hinders student learning, by subject area, 2000

Percentage of 15-year-old students enrolled in schools where principals report that learning is hindered "to some extent" or "a lot" by a shortage/inadequacy of teachers in the following subject areas:

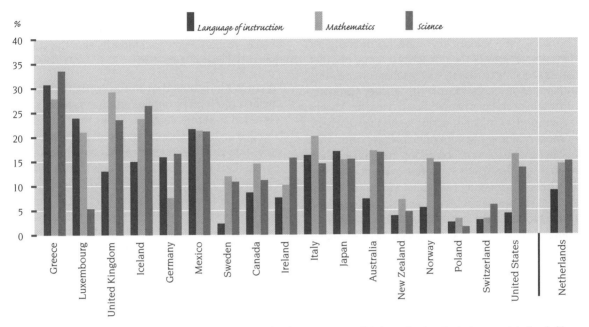

Note: Only countries for which the perception of principals on whether shortages in general hinder student learning is above a certain threshold are considered. The threshold is defined as the sum of "to some extent" or "a lot" responses being 8% for shortages in general (indicator shown in Figure 3.1). Countries are ordered, from left to right, according to the value of that sum.

For the Netherlands, the response rate is too low to ensure comparability.

Source: OECD PISA database at *www.pisa.oecd.org* ....

Data for Figure 3.2, p. 87.

It should be borne in mind that such reports may well be influenced by cross-cultural differences in how principals interpret a "shortage/inadequacy of teachers". For example, principals in countries generally less affected by a teacher shortage/ inadequacy may consider a modest level of shortages as having an important impact on student learning, whereas principals in countries with more serious shortage problems may see things differently. Moreover, although principals are obviously well placed to provide information about their own school, they are a single source of information. Nevertheless, the information obtained from school principals is instructive.

In half of the countries, principals report that learning is hindered at least "a little" by a shortage/ inadequacy of teachers in schools covering at least half of the 15-year-old student population. In the Netherlands, Germany, Greece, the United Kingdom and Mexico, at least two-thirds of students are enrolled in schools where principals thought that there was at least some effect. In contrast, over 65% of students in Spain, Austria and Switzerland are enrolled in schools where principals thought there was no effect.

Another issue of interest is how principals perceive the relative effect of a teacher shortage/ inadequacy by subject area. Figure 3.2 provides strong indications that, for countries in which general shortages/inadequacies are perceived as more problematic, the shortage/inadequacy problem is seen by principals as hindering student learning more severely in mathematics and science

---

3. The country-level averages shown are based on relating principals' responses to students who completed the PISA reading literacy assessment; similar results apply to the mathematics and science assessments.

than in the language of instruction. This is particularly the case in Australia, Iceland, Norway, Sweden, the United Kingdom and the United States.

It is important to put these principals' perceptions about teacher shortage/inadequacy in context. The 2000 PISA survey also asked principals for their perceptions of the impact of a range of other aspects relating to teachers: (i) teachers not meeting individual students' needs; (ii) teacher turnover; (iii) low expectations of teachers; (iv) teacher absenteeism; and (v) students lacking respect for teachers. In most countries, school principals reported that teacher shortages were not among the main teacher-related factors directly hindering student learning. Teachers not meeting individual students' needs, student discipline problems, and students lacking respect for teachers emerged as larger concerns. Of course, there may be knock-on effects of teacher shortage/inadequacy that influence these other factors. For example, if many temporary teachers are used, this could influence discipline problems and student respect.

Outcomes of recruitment processes

A direct way to assess the difficulty experienced by schools in recruiting qualified teachers is to consider measurable aspects of recruitment outcomes, including the number of unfilled vacancies, the number of "difficult to fill" vacancies, the proportion of vacancies "unfilled" for a significant period of time, the proportion of positions filled by teachers without regular qualifications, and the number of applicants for positions.

Comparable international data on these shortage indicators are not readily available. However, some countries conduct surveys on the recruitment of qualified teachers which, although not strictly comparable, provide useful insights. The available data show that the situation differs substantially among countries. While some seem to be facing difficulties in hiring qualified teachers, others appear to have a large pool of qualified applicants.

Figure 3.3 provides information on unfilled teaching vacancies in England and Wales, New Zealand and the Netherlands. These indicators suggest some concerns with teacher recruitment. For instance, around one in seven regular new teaching positions in Dutch secondary schools were not filled when the

2000 school year started, which was over twice the rate in 1997 (Figure 3.3A). Using a different measure, in New Zealand, 1.5% of all secondary posts were unfilled at the commencement of the school year, in January 2002 (Figure 3.3B). In England, for the school year 2000-01, 1.4% of all teaching posts were not filled by January, some four months after the start of the school year (Figure 3.3C).

Figure 3.3 indicates that in the Netherlands and England the level of unfilled teacher vacancies has worsened in recent years, and less markedly so in New Zealand. In addition, the extent of the problem varies across at least three dimensions. It tends to be more serious: (i) in secondary schools than in primary schools; (ii) in specific regions of the country (*e.g.* in London in the case of England, and in the west of the Netherlands); and (iii) in specific subject areas such as mathematics and information technology (Figure 3.3D). In New Zealand, unfilled teacher vacancies are more likely in rural areas than in other locations, and in schools with larger proportions of students from low socio-economic backgrounds (Ministry of Education, New Zealand, 2002).

Nevertheless, some signs suggest that teacher recruitment problems are not general across the OECD area. For instance, in Japan, the 2001 results of the yearly teacher appointment examination reveal that only 6% of qualified examinees were appointed as teachers in lower secondary education, which suggests a large pool of eligible applicants. The figures for primary and upper secondary education were 11% and 7%, respectively.[4] Likewise, in France, in the 2000 teacher recruitment national competition, only 21% of candidates were admitted into the profession (Ministère de l'Éducation Nationale, France, 2002).

Flows out of the profession

Important measures for characterising problems associated with teacher supply are the levels of teacher turnover and attrition.[5] These measures

---

4. Data provided by the Ministry of Education, Culture, Sports, Science and Technology of Japan.

5. Turnover and attrition have distinct meanings throughout this chapter. Turnover refers to those teachers who leave their current teaching position, including those that transfer to different teaching jobs in other schools, while attrition refers to those teachers who leave the teaching profession altogether. Attrition is a subset of turnover.

Figure 3.3 Unfilled teaching vacancies – The Netherlands, New Zealand, England and Wales
(Note that the scale used is different for each figure)

A *Percentage of unfilled teaching vacancies, the Netherlands,
by level of education and region, 1997 and 2000*

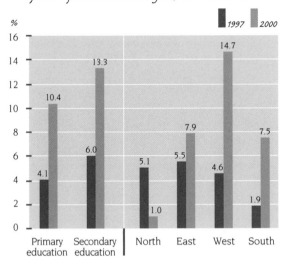

Figures correspond to the percentage of regular vacancies unfilled at
the beginning of the school year, relative to the total number of regular
vacancies before the school year.

Source: Ministry of Education, Culture and Science, the Netherlands
(2002). ....

B *Percentage of unfilled teaching vacancies, New Zealand,
by level of education, 2001 and 2002*

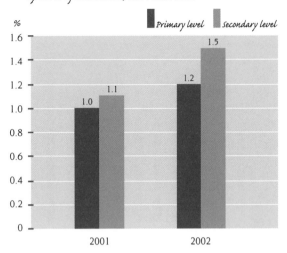

Figures correspond to open positions not filled by a permanent teacher
or long-term reliever as a proportion of all positions in a school that
are funded by the government.

Source: Ministry of Education, New Zealand (2002). ....

C *Percentage of unfilled teaching vacancies, England and
Wales, by region of country, 1999 and 2001*

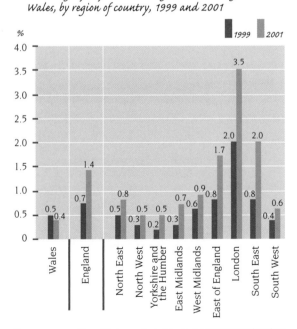

Figures correspond to unfilled vacancies in January as a percentage of teachers
in post for the respective region, in publicly funded nursery, primary, secondary
and special schools.

Source: Department for Education and Skills (2001). ....

D *Percentage of unfilled teaching vacancies, England and
Wales, by subject area, secondary level, 1996 and 2001*

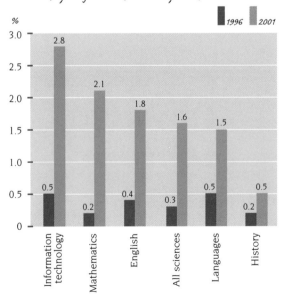

Figures correspond to unfilled vacancies in January as a percentage of
teachers in post for the respective subject area in publicly funded secondary
schools.

Source: Department for Education and Skills (2001). ....

THE TEACHING WORKFORCE:
CONCERNS AND POLICY CHALLENGES

Figure 3.4 Teacher turnover and attrition rates – England, New Zealand and the United States
(Note that the scale used is different for each figure)

A *Turnover rate, England, all schools for full-time service in the publicly funded school sector, 1998-99*

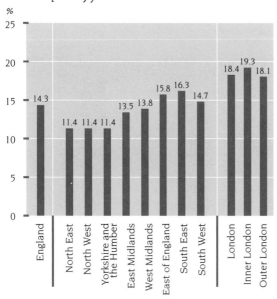

B *Loss rates of regular teachers, New Zealand, 1996-97 to 2000-01*

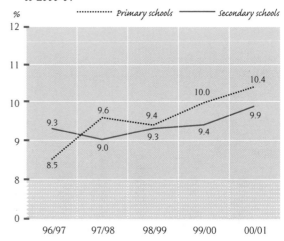

Turnover rate is defined as the proportion of all teachers in full-time service in the English publicly funded schools sector on 31 March 1998 who were not in full-time service in the same establishment on 31 March 1999. It therefore includes individuals leaving the profession and transfers to other establishments.

Source: Department for Education and Skills (2001). ....

Loss rate is defined as the yearly rate at which permanent full-time and part-time teachers leave the New Zealand School State System. Losses include individuals deciding to teach overseas or in private schools, teachers moving to limited term appointments and teachers on leave without pay.

Source: Data provided by the Ministry of Education, New Zealand. ....

C *Teacher attrition by years of experience, United States, 1994-95*

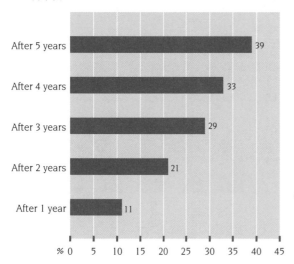

D *Turnover rate, United States, by type of activity*

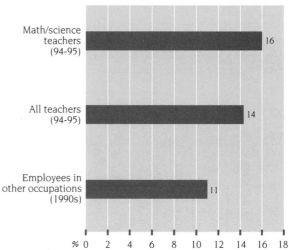

The figures correspond to the cumulative percentage of beginning teachers having left the teaching occupation by 1994-95.

Source: Figure reproduced from Ingersoll (2002*a*)...................................

Turnover rate is defined as the yearly rate at which workers leave their current employment position. It includes employment movements within the same occupation – transfers to a different post in another workplace – and **attrition** – those who leave the occupation altogether.

Source: Figure reproduced from Ingersoll (2002*b*). ....

are more informative when considered alongside inflow rates of new recruits and changes in the size of the student-age population, but their change over time and regional or subject-matter specificity help to characterise retention issues. Countries differ markedly in the general level of teacher attrition:

- England, with 9% for all schools in 1999-2000 (Department for Education and Skills, 2001);

- The Netherlands, with 7% for primary schools in 2000 (Ministry of Education, Culture and Science, the Netherlands, 2002);

- Australia, with 5% for secondary and 4% for primary teachers in 1999 (Ministerial Council on Employment, Education, Training and Youth Affairs, 2001);

- Germany, with 5% for all schools in 1999/2000 (Federal Statistical Office, Germany, 2001);

- Canada, with 2.4% for all schools, on average, between 1988 and 1998 (Gervais and Thony, 2001);

- Japan, with around 2-3% in 1997 (see footnote 4); and

- Korea, with around 2% in 2001 (Ministry of Education and Human Resources Development, Republic of Korea, 2001).

Figure 3.4 shows data on turnover and attrition rates. The rates vary markedly among regions within countries. For instance, in England, turnover rates are considerably higher in the London area than in other regions (Figure 3.4A). In some countries, turnover or attrition rates have been rising over time. The case of New Zealand is shown in Figure 3.4B, where the attrition rate among government primary school teachers rose from 8.5% to 10.4% between 1996-97 and 2000-01, and for secondary schools from 9.3% to 9.9%.[6] Teacher attrition rates are cumulative in their impact. As Figure 3.4C shows for the United States in the mid-1990s, although attrition rates tend to decline the longer that teachers are in the profession, around 39% of the intake to teaching had left the profession after five years. Figure 3.4D also shows that, in the United States, turnover rates for teachers, and particularly for mathematics and science teachers, are above those of employees in other occupations.

Figure 3.5 provides information on the destinations of leavers and the reasons given by teachers for leaving their job in England and Wales in 2001, and in the United States in 1994-95. Interestingly, while in both countries concerns about working conditions and school climate figured prominently among the reasons that teachers provided, significant differences emerge regarding the dominant reason. Those in the United States nominated poor salaries as the main reason for leaving, whereas British teachers emphasised the heavy workload.

An important issue is whether attrition is mostly retirement-related or not. The data available show that this depends on the country concerned. For instance, in Japan for 1997, 60% of all teachers who left the profession did so because of retirement. Similarly, in France, according to the Ministère de l'Éducation Nationale (2001), 78% of secondary school teachers are expected to leave within the period 2000-09 because of retirement. In other countries, the figures for retirement-related attrition are considerably lower: around 12% in New Zealand (2001); 38% and 23% in Australia in primary and secondary schools, respectively (1999); 34% in England in secondary schools (2001); and 11% in the United States in 1994-95.[7] Clearly, in some countries retention is a major consideration as a substantial number of teachers leave the profession for reasons other than retirement.

Teacher qualifications

An indication of the adequacy of the teaching workforce can also be provided by the qualifications of the current stock of teachers. The 2000 PISA survey asked secondary school principals how many teachers were fully qualified by the appropriate authority.[8] In over half of the OECD countries, more than 90% of the full-time secondary teaching workforce was reported as

---

6. Similar data, not shown in Figure 3.4, indicate that between 1996 and 1999 teacher attrition rates increased in Australia from 3% to 4% in primary schools and from 4% to 5% in secondary schools. In the Netherlands, teacher attrition rates in primary schools rose from 4% to 7% between 1996 and 2000.

7. As retirement schemes differ considerably across countries, comparisons of retirement-related attrition rates should take into account the specific national contexts.

8. These data rely on principals' definitions and judgements of who is a qualified teacher, which may vary across countries.

THE TEACHING WORKFORCE:
CONCERNS AND POLICY CHALLENGES

Figure 3.5 Destinations of teachers who leave their position, and reasons for leaving – England and Wales, and the United States

A *Destinations of teachers who leave their current teaching position, England and Wales, secondary education, Summer 2001*

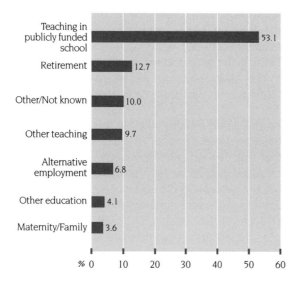

Source: Smithers and Robinson (2001).

B *Reasons for turnover according to teachers, United States, 1994-95*

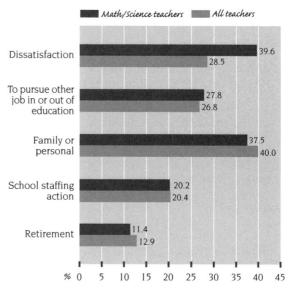

Note: Respondents could indicate more than one reason and so figures add up to more than 100% for each category of teachers.
Source: Figure reproduced from Ingersoll (2002b).

C *Reasons given by teachers for resigning, England and Wales, secondary education, Summer 2001*

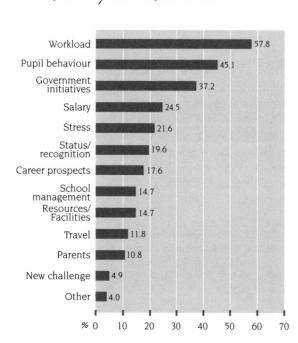

Note: Respondents could indicate more than one reason and so figures add up to more than 100%.
Source: Smithers and Robinson (2001).

D *Reasons for dissatisfaction-related turnover given by teachers, United States, 1994-95*

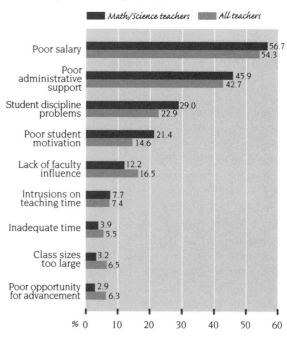

Note: Respondents could indicate more than one reason and so figures add up to more than 100% for each category of teachers.
Source: Figure reproduced from Ingersoll (2002b).

| Figure 3.6 | Qualifications of teachers, United States and Australia |

A *Percentage of teachers without regular certification, United States, public schools, by type of enrolment and community, 1993-94*

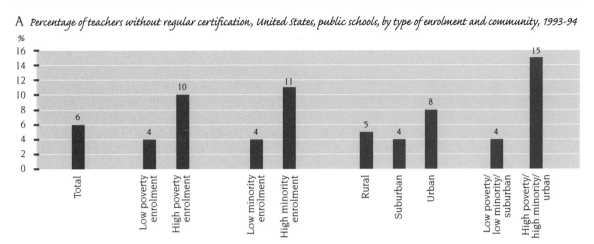

Source: Ingersoll (2002c).

B *Percentage of teachers without a major in subject taught, Australia, secondary schools, 1999*

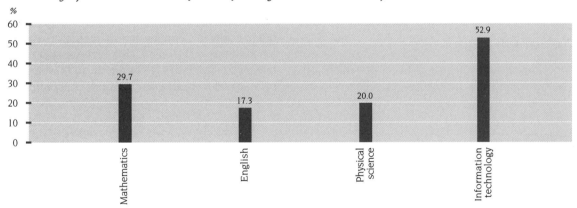

Source: Ministerial Council on Employment, Education, Training and Youth Affairs (2001).

C *Percentage of public high school teachers without a major or minor in course taught, United States, 1993-94 and 1999-2000*

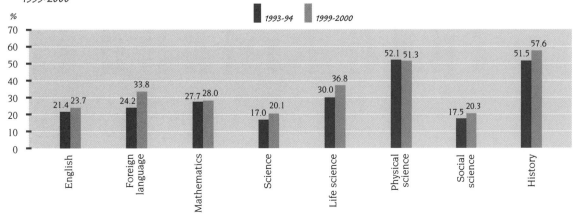

Source: U.S. Department of Education (2002).

THE TEACHING WORKFORCE:
CONCERNS AND POLICY CHALLENGES

fully qualified (OECD PISA database, 2001). In this respect, the situation seems to be more problematic in Portugal, New Zealand, Luxembourg and Mexico, where less than 80% of full-time secondary teachers were reported as fully qualified.

Figure 3.6 provides information from other sources on the qualifications of teachers in the United States (1993-94 and 1999-2000) and Australia (1999). As can be seen from Figure 3.6A, in the United States teacher qualification status tends to differ depending on the type of enrolment and community. In particular, the percentage of teachers with no regular certification status is greater in high-poverty, urban and high-minority enrolment schools. Figures 3.6B and 3.6C show that for Australia and the United States respectively, the percentage of secondary teachers without a qualification in the subject taught was strikingly high for some subjects (particularly mathematics, physical science and information technology).

Age distribution of teachers

One important indicator of likely pressures on teacher supply is the proportion of teachers who are in their 50s and thus approaching retirement age. There is no single rule about what is an appropriate proportion in each age-band, given that typical entry and exit ages vary by country. However, within each country, a growing percentage of older teachers can potentially create staffing difficulties through increased retirement rates. As Figures 3.7 and 3.8 show, in 2000 several countries had a very high percentage of teachers aged over 50 years, particularly in secondary education. Around 50% of the teachers in German and Italian lower-secondary schools were aged over 50 years. About 40% of teachers were in this age group in Swedish and German primary schools. However, in other countries, notably Austria, Korea and Portugal, there was no such skewing towards older teachers.

Figures 3.7 and 3.8 show, for primary and lower secondary teachers respectively, how the teaching force aged quite markedly during the 1990s. Between 1992 and 2000, the proportion of teachers aged over 50 years rose sharply in some countries – most dramatically in Germany, from a quarter to almost a half in just eight years. It also rose substantially in New Zealand, the Netherlands and Sweden in primary education, and in France, Italy and the

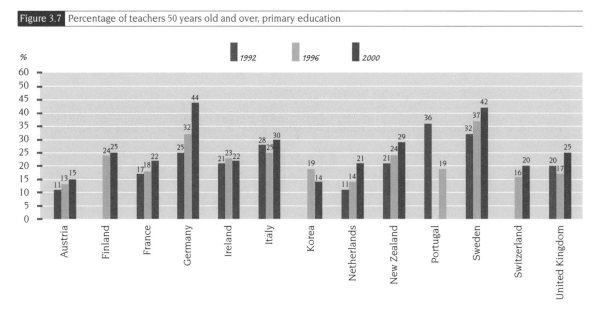

Figure 3.7 Percentage of teachers 50 years old and over, primary education

Note: While data for 2000 include private and public sectors, data for 1992 and 1996 are limited to the public sector. 1992 data for France, Ireland and the United Kingdom and 2000 data for the Netherlands include pre-primary sector. Data for 1992 for Germany refer to the former Federal Rep. of Germany and include government-dependent private institutions. 2000 data for Switzerland include only public institutions. The 1992 figure for the United Kingdom is limited to England and Wales while the 1996 figure is limited to England and Scotland. The 2000 figures for Austria and Switzerland refer to 1999.

Source: OECD (1995, 1998) and OECD Education Database, 2002.

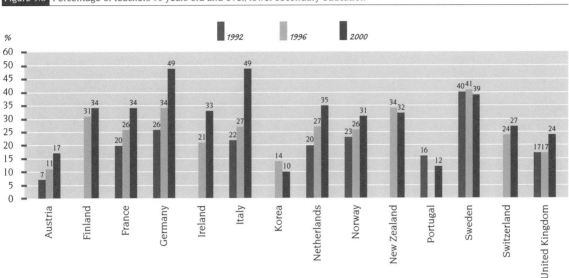

Figure 3.8 Percentage of teachers 50 years old and over, lower secondary education

Note: While data for 2000 include private and public sectors, data for 1992 and 1996 are limited to the public sector. 1992 data for France, the Netherlands, Portugal and the United Kingdom, 1996 data for Ireland and New Zealand, and 2000 data for Ireland and the Netherlands include upper secondary sector. Data for 1992 for Germany refer to the former Federal Rep. of Germany and include government-dependent private institutions. 2000 data for Switzerland include only public institutions and 2000 data for Norway include primary level. The 1992 figure for the United Kingdom is limited to England and Wales while the 1996 figure is limited to England and Scotland. The 2000 figures for Austria and Switzerland refer to 1999.

Source: OECD (1995, 1998) and OECD Education Database, 2002.

Netherlands in lower secondary education. In other countries, there was a less pronounced "ageing" trend (Ireland, Austria, Switzerland for both sectors, France in primary education), while Korea and Portugal showed no marked trend in this direction.

An increase in the average age of the teaching workforce can have several effects. First, it generally has budgetary implications since in most school systems there is a link between pay and years of teaching experience (although in some systems teachers' salaries peak quite early in their careers). Second, although a more experienced teaching workforce can bring benefits to schools, it can also be the case that additional resources are needed to update skills, knowledge and motivation among those who have been teaching for a long time. Third, unless appropriate action to train and recruit more teachers is already underway, shortages are likely if the proportion of teachers retiring remains high or continues to rise.

Relative salaries

Teacher supply is affected by the relative attractiveness of the profession. However, despite the

prominence that teachers' relative salaries play in debates about the attractiveness of teaching, there are only limited internationally comparable data available. The main indicator that is currently used, teachers' statutory salary expressed as a ratio of GDP per capita, has a number of limitations,[9] and is not available over time for all Member countries.

Figure 3.9 shows what happened to this ratio between 1994 and 2000 for teachers in lower secondary education with 15 years of teaching experience.[10] The trend is clear. In every country,

---

9. The indicator is limited because it is based on statutory rather than actual salaries, financial benefits other than salaries are not included, and the reference point, GDP per capita, does not reflect salary levels in comparable occupations. A more appropriate indicator would compare teachers' actual salaries and other benefits with those of workers in professions requiring similar qualifications and at similar age levels. Such data are not yet available at international level. The OECD is working with Member countries to improve the international data on teacher salaries and other working conditions.

10. Similar changes in relative salary levels to those shown in Figure 3.9 are also evident for primary and upper secondary teachers in the countries that report such data.

Figure 3.9 | Ratio of teachers' statutory salaries after 15 years of experience to GDP per capita, public institutions, lower secondary education

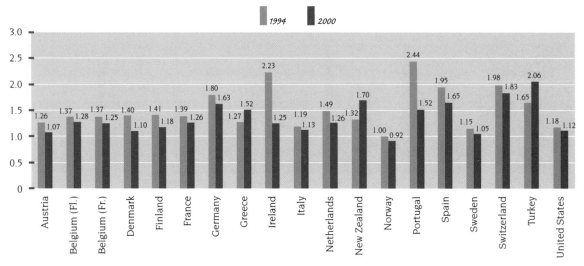

Note: For 1994, common data were used for both Belgian Communities. For Turkey, the figures refer to primary education. All OECD countries for which data are available for both years considered are shown.
Source: OECD (1996, 2001a, 2002).

except Greece, New Zealand and Turkey, the statutory salaries of such teachers relative to GDP per capita have declined. In some cases, such as Ireland, Portugal and Spain, the decline was very steep over the six-year period. However, it should be borne in mind that this measure is an imperfect one.

Size of the school-age population

Figures 3.10 and 3.11 provide information on the expected changes in the size of the school-aged population from 2000 to 2010 in OECD countries for the age groups 5-14 and 15-19, respectively. These data indicate one aspect of the likely demand for teachers over this period. For the 5-14 age range, which broadly covers primary and lower secondary education, 23 countries are expecting a decline between 2000 and 2010 (Figure 3.10). Substantial declines of over 20% are projected for the Czech Republic, Hungary, Poland, the Slovak Republic, and Sweden. The main exceptions are Turkey, Luxembourg, Japan, and Ireland where small increases are projected, and Korea, Mexico and New Zealand where the 2010 population of 5-14 year-olds is expected to be around the same size as in 2000.

For the age group 15-19, which broadly corresponds with upper secondary education, the population projections reveal more mixed results (Figure 3.11).

Of the 30 Member countries, 16 are projected to see a decline by 2010, with declines of over 20% projected for Greece, Ireland, Poland, and Spain. However, 13 countries are projected to see an increase by 2010, with rises of over 10% projected for Denmark, Luxembourg, Norway and Sweden. To the extent that education participation rates among 15-19 year-olds rise between 2000 and 2010, these population projections may understate the numbers enrolled in upper secondary education by 2010. As seen earlier, it is generally in upper secondary education that the recruitment challenges implied by an ageing teaching force are likely to be most marked.

3. POLICY TOOLS AND CHALLENGES

In considering possible policy responses, governments need to take account of the kinds of evidence presented in this chapter about the linked nature of the problem – teaching quality is likely to suffer when there is inadequate supply. The potentially wide range of policy tools involved is summarised in Table 3.1 and elaborated in OECD (2001c).

An important area for intervention relates to the determination of the number of teachers needed to respond to the educational needs of a given student population. At this level, educational

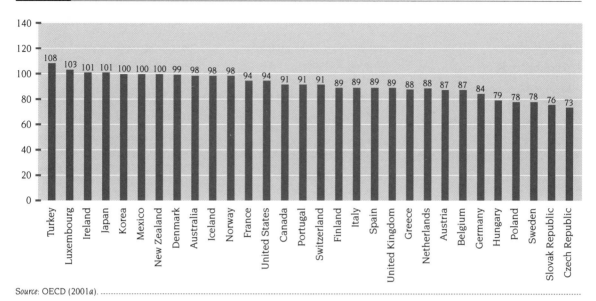

Figure 3.10 Expected changes in the school-age population from 2000 to 2010 (2000=100), ages 5-14

Source: OECD (2001*a*).

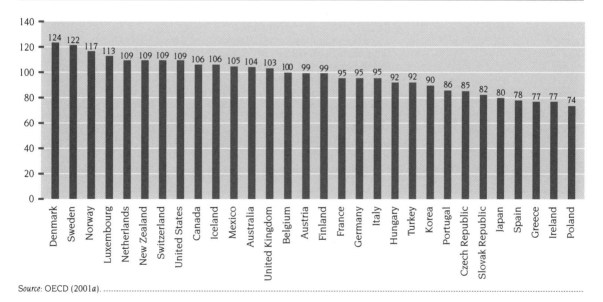

Figure 3.11 Expected changes in the school-age population from 2000 to 2010 (2000=100), ages 15-19

Source: OECD (2001*a*).

authorities can use class size, teaching loads, quantity of instruction, or the number and role of teaching assistants and other support staff, to influence the number of teachers needed. These can be labelled "demand-side" tools. "Supply-side" tools include the structure of teacher education programmes, training more teachers, determining entry requirements to the profession, and making teaching more attractive as a career. Other tools are concerned more with the mechanisms through which demand and supply interact, and are related to the structure of the labour market for teachers. Such "matching process" tools include the definition of bargaining mechanisms, the level of centralisation of bargaining and the recruitment, selection and assignment processes.

Table 3.1 Potential policy tools to manage the teaching workforce

"Demand-side" tools	"Supply-side" tools	"Matching process" tools
– Class size; – Teaching loads; – Required learning time for students; – Use of teaching assistants and other support staff; – Use of technology and distance learning; – Structure of curriculum and educational programmes; – Starting and ending age of compulsory education; – Academic standards defining requirements for graduation.	**Attractiveness of the profession** Monetary incentives – Relative salaries; – Career structure and salary scale; – Other (*e.g.* merit-based awards, signing bonuses, differentiated pay, housing subsidies, childcare, income tax credits). Non-monetary incentives – Vacation time, flexibility to take leave; – Working conditions: opportunities for collaboration and decision-making, school safety and student discipline, class size, working loads, quality of facilities and instructional materials. **Teacher education and certification** Teacher initial education and professional development: Supply, structure, content and accreditation of teacher education programmes; incentives to engage in teacher education; induction and mentoring programmes; provision of professional development activities. Certification of teachers: Definition of certification standards; alternative certification programmes.	**Bargaining mechanisms** Set of mechanisms for bargaining: setting of salaries, pay differentiation to account for shortages, opening of profession to international markets. **Level of centralisation of bargaining** Degree of autonomy of schools regarding: recruitment, selection and assignment of teachers; and setting of incentive structure. **Recruitment and selection processes** Organisation; definition of qualification requirements; delegation of authority to recruit, select and assign teachers; methods for screening candidates; emergency recruitment programmes.

There is little evidence available internationally on the impact of a number of the policy tools outlined in Table 3.1, such as the greater use of other types of personnel in schools, and more school autonomy in setting teachers' salaries and working conditions. The recently launched OECD review is investigating current country experience with such approaches.[11]

Policy making on teachers faces two major difficulties. First, the sheer size and diversity of the teaching force, and the wide range of schools in which they work, suggest that it is difficult to develop policies that can be applied across-the-board with equally effective results. The evidence presented in Section 2 on how shortages vary by subject area, level of schooling and regional location suggests that it may be more productive for policy to focus on the factors that may attract particular types of people into teaching, and teachers to particular schools, than on teacher supply in more generic terms. For example, it seems that experiences in the first few years help determine whether a teacher will have a long career (Stinebrickner, 1999), suggesting that policies countering teacher attrition should focus on relatively recent entrants. Attrition is also greater in certain

---

11. The OECD review is outlined in footnote 2.

academic disciplines, such as science, and for teachers with higher academic credentials (Murnane *et al.*, 1989). Research suggests that women are more likely to leave teaching for family reasons, while men are more likely to leave for alternative careers (Dolton and van der Klaauw, 1999). It would thus be pertinent to increase the attractiveness of teaching to women with disrupted careers, and to provide more supportive services such as childcare. Such findings support the case for targeted teacher policies, and yet there are often pressures for "one size fits all" responses.

A second difficulty is that teacher policy can require some stark trade-offs. Class size provides a clear example. As shown in Table 3.1, class size is a factor on both the demand and the supply sides of the teacher labour market. Most school systems have reduced average class sizes in recent years. Yet the research evidence tends to suggest that, while targeted class size reductions can be beneficial for some students (such as those in the early years of primary education or from disadvantaged backgrounds), across-the-board reductions in class size are expensive and unlikely to lead to substantial learning gains (Hanushek, 2000; Hoxby, 2000; Meuret, 2001). Indeed, there could even be a case for using an increase in average class size to fund higher teacher salaries and thereby make teaching more attractive to higher quality candidates.[12] However, the size of classes also affects teachers' working conditions, and teachers faced with larger classes may become more dissatisfied and inclined to leave the profession, thereby worsening supply. One of the few studies to look at this aspect (Mont and Rees, 1996) found that in the United States high schools with above-average class sizes were associated with a higher resignation rate of teachers. On the other hand, Stinebrickner (1999) concluded that, while the student-teacher ratio (which is highly correlated with class size) plays a significant role in whether teachers consider a school to be desirable, it is less important than salary.

Salary questions figure prominently in debates on teacher policy. The research reviewed in OECD (2001c) suggests that pay can influence:

– *The decision to become a teacher*: For example, Dolton (1990) found that graduates' choices in the

United Kingdom were associated with relative earnings in teaching and non-teaching occupations, and their likely growth.

– *The decision to remain in teaching*: Research from the United States and the United Kingdom suggests that not only do teachers who are paid more stay in teaching longer, but also that those who are likely to be able to get higher-paid jobs outside teaching, as indicated by their educational qualifications or test scores, have on average shorter teaching careers (Murnane and Olsen, 1990; Dolton and van der Klaauw, 1999).

– *The decision to return to teaching after a career interruption*: Only one in four American teachers returns to the classroom within five years of leaving it (Murnane, 1996); returning rates tend to be higher among those teaching subjects that provide fewer opportunities for employment elsewhere (Beaudin, 1993).

It would seem that the main linkages between teacher salaries and quality apply at two points. One is where the financial attractiveness of teaching relative to other professions influences the pool of people who consider teaching as a career: the higher teacher salaries, the larger this pool is likely to be and, therefore, the higher the likely quality of those available for employment as teachers. The second point is in terms of the incentive structures facing those currently in teaching – salary progression, the length of the salary scale, and promotion opportunities. Some salary structures reward formal qualifications and years spent in teaching rather than those teacher characteristics which, although harder to measure – enthusiasm, commitment and sensitivity to student needs – may be more directly related to the quality of teaching and learning.

---

12. Correspondingly, a policy to improve outcomes by reducing class size may fail if it results in the hiring of teachers of lower quality. This appears to have occurred in the class-size reduction programme in California which started in 1996 to reduce the size of all classes in the first three years of primary school from an average of 30 students to a maximum of 20 students. Improved student behaviour and learning was evident in the reduced classes but the gains have been fairly small, in part because teachers did not always adapt their teaching behaviour to capitalise on the smaller classes, and because the increased demand has led to a shortage of qualified teachers (Stecher *et al.*, 2001).

Despite the undoubted importance of salary issues, they form just part of the policy package, as Table 3.1 makes clear. Educational authorities in those countries more seriously affected by shortfalls face the following challenges: to design incentives to attract high-quality candidates and former teachers to the pool of those who want to teach; exclude from the pool those who lack the skills to teach; and retain and further develop the skills of those effective teachers currently in the profession. Policies aimed at attracting and retaining effective teachers need both to recruit able people into the profession, and also to provide support and incentives for on-going performance at high levels and professional growth. Teachers are not necessarily going to reach their full potential in settings that do not provide appropriate support, or sufficient challenge and recognition.

4. CONCLUSION

This chapter has used the currently available data to review some of the policy issues concerning the teaching workforce in OECD countries, especially in regard to actual or looming shortfalls in teacher supply.

Several things are clear. First, measuring the nature and extent of teacher shortages is difficult. Agreed indicators do not yet exist at international level, and there is uneven coverage of available data among OECD countries. A large part of the difficulty arises because a teacher shortage raises quality as well as quantity issues. Even though a school system may have few, if any, unstaffed classrooms, problems with teacher recruitment may still have necessitated responses that raise concerns about the quality of teaching. The lack of comparative international information on teacher shortages, their causes and effects, has been a major factor in launching the new OECD project.

Second, the limited but suggestive data available provide indications that some countries are currently experiencing difficulties in recruiting and retaining qualified teachers. In such countries there are indications that: (i) there is a sizeable proportion of unfilled vacancies; (ii) attrition and turnover rates have increased in recent years; (iii) the proportion of "out-of-field" teaching assignments is high in some key subject areas; (iv) the age profile of teachers is skewed towards the upper end of the age-range; and (v) school principals report that a teacher shortage/inadequacy is hindering student learning. Other countries, however, still seem to have relatively large pools of qualified individuals from which to recruit. These countries may still consider teacher quality to be an issue, but not because of shortages of qualified staff.

Third, the problems of teacher shortages are uneven. Shortages tend to be more marked in certain subject areas such as science, mathematics, information technology or foreign languages in secondary education, and in some specific regions within countries.

Teacher policy is currently high on the agenda of OECD countries. In addition to general questions to do with the changing roles of teachers and the attractiveness of teaching overall, there are also important issues concerned with the differentiation within the teaching profession, more flexible pathways into teaching, incentive structures rewarding the skills and performance that most closely relate to student learning, as well as teacher evaluation and accountability. The immediate challenges raised in some countries by teacher shortages are helping to open up significant long-term questions about how to improve the quality of teaching and the effectiveness of teachers' work.

References

BEAUDIN, B. (1993), "Teachers who interrupt their careers: characteristics of those who return to the classroom", *Educational Evaluation and Policy Analysis*, Vol. 15, No. 1, pp. 51-64.

CANADIAN TEACHERS' FEDERATION (2000), "Survey of Canadian school boards on supply/demand issues", *Economic Services Bulletin*, October.

DEPARTMENT FOR EDUCATION AND SKILLS (2001), *Statistics of Education: Teachers in England (including teachers' pay for England and Wales)*, London.

DOLTON, P. (1990), "The economics of UK teacher supply: the graduate's decision", *The Economic Journal*, No. 100, pp. 91-104.

DOLTON, P. and **VAN DER KLAAUW, W.** (1999), "The turnover of teachers: a competing risks explanation", *The Review of Economics and Statistics*, Vol. 81, No. 3, pp. 543-552.

EDUCATION COMMISSION OF THE STATES (2001), "Teaching quality", *Elementary and Secondary Education Act (ESEA) Policy Brief*, Denver, Colorado.

FEDERAL STATISTICAL OFFICE GERMANY – STATISTISCHES BUNDESAMT (2001), "Bildung und Kultur (Fachserie 11), Allgemeinbildende Schulen (Reihe 1)", Wiesbaden.

GERVAIS, G. and **THONY, I.** (2001), "The supply and demand of elementary-secondary educators in Canada", presented to the 2001 Pan Canadian Education Research Agenda Symposium, Laval University.

HANUSHEK, E. (2000), "Evidence, politics, and the class size debate", *The Class Size Policy Debate*, Working Paper No. 121, Economic Policy Institute, Washington D.C.

HOXBY, C. (2000), "The effects of class size on student achievement: new evidence from population variation", *The Quarterly Journal of Economics*, Vol. 115, No. 4, pp. 1239:85.

INGERSOLL, R. (1999), "The problem of underqualified teachers in American secondary schools", *Educational Researcher*, Vol. 28, No. 2, pp. 26-37.

INGERSOLL, R. (2002*a*), "The teacher shortage: a case of wrong diagnosis and wrong prescription", NASSP (National Association of Secondary Schools Principals) Bulletin 86, No. 631, United States, pp.16-30.

INGERSOLL, R. (2002*b*), "Turnover and shortages among science teachers in the U.S.", *Science Teacher Retention: Mentoring and Renewal*, National Science Teachers Association and the National Science Education Leadership Association, United States.

INGERSOLL, R. (2002*c*), "Out-of-field teaching, educational inequality, and the organization of schools: an exploratory analysis", Center for the Study of Teaching and Policy, University of Washington.

MEURET, D. (2001), *Les recherches sur la réduction de la taille des classes*, IREDU, Université de Bourgogne, France.

MINISTÈRE DE L'ÉDUCATION NATIONALE, FRANCE (2001), "Les besoins en personnels d'enseignement, d'éducation et d'orientation dans le second degré public entre 2002 et 2009", *Éducation & formations*, No. 58, Janvier-Mars, Paris.

MINISTÈRE DE L'ÉDUCATION NATIONALE, FRANCE (2002), "Concours de recrutement de professeurs des écoles, Session 2000", *Note d'Information*, 02-19, April, Paris.

MINISTERIAL COUNCIL ON EMPLOYMENT, EDUCATION, TRAINING AND YOUTH AFFAIRS (2001), *Demand and Supply of Primary and Secondary School Teachers in Australia*, Melbourne.

MINISTRY OF EDUCATION, NEW ZEALAND (2002), *Monitoring Teacher Supply: Survey of Staffing in New Zealand, Schools at the Beginning of the 2002 School Year*, Wellington.

MINISTRY OF EDUCATION, CULTURE AND SCIENCE, THE NETHERLANDS (2002), *Education and Science in the Netherlands: Facts and Figures*, The Hague.

MINISTRY OF EDUCATION AND HUMAN RESOURCES DEVELOPMENT, REPUBLIC OF KOREA (2001), *Statistical Yearbook of Education*, Korean Educational Development Institute, Seoul.

MONT, D. and REES, D. (1996), "The influence of classroom characteristics on high school teacher turnover", *Economic Inquiry*, Vol. 34, pp. 152-167.

MURNANE, R. (1996), "Staffing the nation's schools with skilled teachers", in E. Hanushek and D. Jorgenson (eds.), *Improving America's Schools: The Role of Incentives*, National Academy Press, Washington, D.C.

MURNANE, R. and OLSEN, R. (1990), "The effects of salaries and opportunity costs on duration in teaching: evidence from North Carolina", *Journal of Human Resources*, Vol. 25, No. 1, pp. 106-124.

MURNANE, R., SINGER, J. and WILLET, J. (1989), "The influences of salaries and opportunity costs of teachers' career choices: evidence from North Carolina", *Harvard Education Review*, Vol. 59, pp. 325-346.

NATIONAL BOARD OF EDUCATION, FINLAND (2000), "Teachers in 2010, anticipatory project to investigate teachers' initial and continuing training needs (OPEPRO)", Helsinki.

OECD (1995), *Education at a Glance: OECD Indicators*, Paris.

OECD (1996), *Education at a Glance: OECD Indicators*, Paris.

OECD (1998), *Education at a Glance: OECD Indicators*, Paris.

OECD (2001*a*), *Education at a Glance: OECD Indicators*, Paris.

OECD (2001*b*), *Knowledge and Skills for Life: First Results from PISA 2000*, Paris.

OECD (2001*c*), "Teacher demand and supply: improving teacher quality and addressing teacher shortages", paper prepared for the Education Committee and forthcoming Working Paper, Directorate for Education, Paris.

OECD (2002), *Education at a Glance: OECD Indicators 2002*, Paris.

PRESTON, B. (2000), "Teacher supply and demand to 2005: projections and context", Report prepared for the Australian Council of Deans of Education, July.

SMITHERS, A. and ROBINSON, P. (2001), "Teachers leaving", Centre for Education and Employment Research, The University of Liverpool.

STECHER, B., BOHRHSTEDT, G., KIRST, M., MCROBBIE, J. and WILLIAMS, T. (2001), "Class size reduction in California: A story of hope, promise and unintended consequences", *Phi Delta Kappan*, May, pp. 670-674.

STINEBRICKNER, T. (1999), "Using latent variables in dynamic, discrete choice models: the effect of school characteristics on teacher decisions", *Research in Labor Economics*, Vol. 18, pp. 141-176.

U.S. DEPARTMENT OF EDUCATION (2002), *Qualifications of the Public School Teacher Workforce: Prevalence of Out-of-Field Teaching 1987-88 to 1999-2000*, Statistical Analysis Report, National Center for Education Statistics, Washington D.C.

WILSON, A. and PEARSON, R. (1993), "The problem of teacher shortages", *Education Economics*, Vol. 1, No. 1, pp. 69-75.

Data for the Figures
CHAPTER 3
Data for Figures 3.3–3.11 are shown on the Figures.

Data for Figure 3.1

Principals' perceptions on whether a shortage/inadequacy of teachers hinders student learning, 2000

	Percentage of 15-year-old students enrolled in schools where principals report that learning is hindered by a shortage/inadequacy of teachers to the following extent:			
	Not at all	A little	Some	A lot
Australia	45.5	36.9	16.7	0.9
Austria	72.6	21.0	6.4	0.0
Belgium (Fl.)	53.2	39.8	5.6	1.4
Canada	53.8	24.4	19.3	2.5
Czech Republic	62.9	29.5	7.1	0.4
Denmark	56.9	40.5	2.6	0.0
Finland	34.5	59.2	6.2	0.0
France	64.0	29.9	6.2	0.0
Germany	30.0	42.6	25.2	2.2
Greece	31.6	16.9	27.6	23.9
Hungary	62.6	30.8	3.8	2.8
Iceland	36.3	35.7	24.8	3.2
Ireland	46.6	32.1	19.5	1.8
Italy	38.6	41.4	19.0	1.0
Japan	41.4	40.0	17.1	1.4
Korea	58.6	33.7	7.1	0.6
Luxembourg	57.5	5.6	36.9	0.0
Mexico	32.6	40.3	20.3	6.8
Netherlands	22.2	59.4	18.5	0.0
New Zealand	46.3	38.1	15.0	0.6
Norway	36.2	50.6	13.3	0.0
Poland	63.1	24.2	7.8	4.9
Portugal	50.2	45.3	4.5	0.0
Spain	72.9	20.2	6.3	0.6
Sweden	33.8	41.5	22.7	2.0
Switzerland	65.4	24.1	10.5	0.0
United Kingdom	32.4	37.0	27.0	3.7
United States	60.9	30.2	8.2	0.7

Notes: Two Member countries, the Slovak Republic and Turkey, did not participate in the 2000 PISA assessments. For the Netherlands the response rate is too low to ensure comparability with other countries.

Source: OECD PISA database at www.pisa.oecd.org

Data for Figure 3.2

Principals' perceptions on whether a shortage/inadequacy of teachers hinders student learning, by subject area, 2000

	Percentage of 15-year-old students enrolled in schools where principals report that learning is hindered "to some extent" or "a lot" by a shortage/inadequacy of teachers in the following subject areas:		
	Language of instruction	Mathematics	Science
Australia	7.2	17.1	16.8
Canada	8.7	14.5	11.3
Germany	15.8	7.5	16.6
Greece	30.7	27.9	33.6
Iceland	15.0	23.8	26.5
Ireland	7.6	10.2	15.8
Italy	16.2	20.1	14.5
Japan	16.9	15.4	15.4
Luxembourg	23.9	21.1	5.4
Mexico	21.7	21.4	21.3
Netherlands	9.0	14.4	15.1
New Zealand	3.9	7.1	4.7
Norway	5.4	15.5	14.8
Poland	2.4	3.2	1.5
Sweden	2.3	12.0	11.0
Switzerland	2.8	3.2	6.1
United Kingdom	13.0	29.2	23.6
United States	4.3	16.4	13.7

Notes: Only countries for which the perception of principals on whether shortages in general hinder student learning is above a certain threshold are reported in this table. The threshold is defined as the sum of "to some extent" and "a lot" responses being 8% for shortages in general (the indicator shown in Figure 3.1). Two Member countries, the Slovak Republic and Turkey, did not participate in the 2000 PISA assessments. For the Netherlands the response rate is too low to ensure comparability with other countries.

Source: OECD PISA database at www.pisa.oecd.org

.

chapter 4

THE GROWTH OF CROSS-BORDER EDUCATION

▼

SUMMARY

International trade in educational services is growing in importance, particularly in post-secondary education. It can take several forms, including students travelling to study in foreign countries, educational institutions operating abroad, and educational services being supplied across borders through e-learning. This chapter reviews developments and discusses their policy implications.

Growth has been driven partly by demand. International study can broaden students' horizons, and can provide forms of education that are unavailable in their home country. In particular, OECD countries and especially English-speaking ones are able to cater for a growing demand from emerging economies. The motive for supplying these services is also in part cultural, but increasingly there is a commercial motive, with foreign students providing a significant source of revenue.

Growth has also been fostered by the emergence of new forms of supply, whether through the development by academic institutions of campuses in other countries or new possibilities for selling services at a distance through e-learning. At the same time, trade negotiations under the General Agreement on Trade in Services (GATS) are seeking to remove barriers to educational trade.

These developments imply that OECD countries face a more complex policy environment with a wider range of education and training providers, increased connectivity and interdependence among national education systems, and pressure for greater coherence among the national frameworks of post-secondary education. In particular, three issues – student access, funding/regulation, and quality assurance – that are already central to national debates about post-secondary education, now need to be confronted in an international context.

1. INTRODUCTION

There has been rapid growth in the number of students enrolled in educational institutions outside their home country. At the same time, educational providers are increasingly operating overseas, selling services to foreign students who remain at home. Educational services are thus becoming increasingly cross-border or trans-national in both their consumption and their provision. Although there has long been international mobility of students and teachers, a range of factors is increasing the pace at which educational services are crossing national borders. These developments are particularly evident at the post-secondary level of education.[1]

The rising worldwide demand for post-secondary education cannot always be met by domestic institutions, especially in developing countries. Moreover, students increasingly perceive that they can gain particular advantages from studying in another country: cultural enrichment and language skills; high-status qualifications; and access to better jobs. Declines in the costs of international travel and communications make it easier for students to study overseas, and to access international educational services while living in their home country. Governments, too, are more actively promoting students' and teachers' international mobility for a mix of cultural, political, labour market and trade reasons. Public and private suppliers of education increasingly see foreign students as sources of revenue, and compete strongly for them. They also employ teachers from a variety of countries to lift institutional quality and enrich students' learning opportunities. The growing transnational nature of education is driven by both demand-side and supply-side forces.

The increasing mobility of students and education programmes across national borders forms part of a wider development that is often termed the "internationalisation" of education. An international perspective is evident in a range of domains including educational structures, curriculum content, and teaching styles in different national settings, as well as the educational objective of expanding students' awareness of the wider world. The process of internationalisation is accelerated when students move to study in another country, or use e-learning technology to access courses from overseas institutions.

Enrolments of non-nationals have been growing at a faster rate than domestic enrolments in the OECD as a whole over recent years. Foreign students represent an important source of export revenue in some OECD countries. They incur large expenditure for their travel expenses, education costs and living expenses. This expenditure amounted to an estimated minimum of US$30 billion in 1998 (Larsen *et al.*, 2002). Most of the expenditure is financed directly by students and their families, although some is met by grants and subsidies from government and private sources.

It is not always necessary for students to move to another country to access that country's educational services. The various forms of trade in educational services are categorised in Table 4.1. They comprise:

– The supply of a service, such as software or distance education, across an international border ("Mode 1" in the terminology used in Table 4.1);

---

1. "Post-secondary education" refers to courses leading to qualifications at a higher level than the end of upper secondary school. In terms of the International Standard Classification of Education (ISCED) of 1997, post-secondary education encompasses: post-secondary non-tertiary education (ISCED 4), the first stage of tertiary education (ISCED 5), which includes university undergraduate degrees and advanced vocational qualifications; and advanced research qualifications (ISCED 6). More details on these classifications are provided in *Education at a Glance – OECD Indicators*. As used in this chapter, the term post-secondary also encompasses adult learning programmes that do not necessarily lead to formal qualifications. The currently available data on cross-border consumption and provision are uneven in their coverage of the full variety of different institutions and courses in post-secondary education. Almost all of the cross-border data refer to the "tertiary education" component of post-secondary education, namely ISCED levels 5 and 6. Within tertiary education, there tends to be more extensive information on university courses than on other types of tertiary study. However, in other instances the national data do not always clearly distinguish the levels of education to which the data apply. The OECD is working with Member countries to improve the scope and quality of internationally available data on the consumption and provision of education services across national borders.

Table 4.1 Main modes of the international supply of educational services			
Mode	**Explanation**	**Education examples**	**Size/potential of market**
1 Cross-border supply.	The provision of a service where the service crosses the border (does not require the physical movement of the consumer).	• Distance education. • Virtual education institutions. • Education software. • Corporate training through ICT delivery.	Currently a relatively small but rapidly growing market. Seen to have great potential through the use of ICT and especially the Internet.
2 Consumption abroad.	Provision of the service involving the movement of the consumer to the country of the supplier.	Students who go to another country to study.	Probably represents the largest share of the current global market for post-secondary educational services.
3 Commercial presence.	The service provider establishes or uses facilities in another country to provide the service.	• Local university or satellite campuses. • Language training companies. • Private training companies.	Growing interest and strong potential for future growth.
4 Presence of natural persons.	Person travelling to another country on a temporary basis to provide the service.	Professors, teachers, researchers working abroad.	Potentially a strong market given the emphasis on mobility of professionals.

Note: The "Mode" and "Explanation" columns are based on the classification used by the General Agreement on Trade in Services (GATS).

– Travel by a student to another country to study (Mode 2);

– The presence in a country of a foreign supplier of a service, such as a training company or an off-shore campus (Mode 3);

– The temporary travel of someone supplying education, such as a professor working abroad (Mode 4).

Most policy attention has so far been directed to studying abroad (Mode 2), which is the dominating mode of trade in education. This is also the form for which data are the most readily available. Fewer data are available for "cross-border supply"

of education service or "commercial presence" (*e.g.* through direct investment in satellite campuses or local affiliates), although these forms appear to be growing rapidly and potentially represent large markets. For example, about 35% of the overseas higher education students enrolled in Australia are based in their home country and study their Australian courses through distance education technology (Mode 1) or at a local education institution (Mode 3). The growth potential for such trade may even be higher than for students moving abroad, stimulated by the use of ICT and the growing interest of private and public institutions and enterprises in these forms of provision.

If these forms of trade continue to grow, this will not only have important economic repercussions, it could also have profound consequences for education, which has traditionally been organised at a national or sub-national level. It could become harder for national governments to use their own post-secondary systems purely to manage the development of their own labour force and to restrict institutional structures and qualifications systems to a national framework. This creates a strong policy interest, which is brought into sharper focus by the negotiations under the General Agreement on Trade in Services (GATS). These negotiations, which resumed in 2000 under the auspices of the World Trade Organization (WTO), could imply a greater liberalisation of trade in post-secondary education over the medium or long term, with fewer barriers to the cross-border supply of educational services and direct investment from overseas in educational provision. Even without the GATS, however, it is highly likely that trade in educational services will continue to grow since much of it takes place outside the WTO framework and is not reflected in GATS commitments.

This chapter highlights some of the key developments in transnational post-secondary education, especially with regard to trade. It starts by looking at the trends in student mobility, in terms of the volume of enrolments, their financial value, and the rationale for foreign study. It then considers the development of other forms of trade in educational services, including the emergence of new providers. Third, it reviews how the GATS negotiations are seeking to remove barriers to such trade, and the potential consequences for national education systems. Fourth, it looks at recent trends in international quality assurance and accreditation. Finally, it discusses emerging policy issues concerning student access, funding and quality assurance arising from the increasingly international character of post-secondary education.

2. STUDENT MOBILITY: FROM A CULTURAL TO A FINANCIAL FOCUS?

Since the early 1950s, a number of OECD countries have encouraged their nationals to travel abroad to study, and have themselves hosted overseas students. Initially this was done for primarily cultural and political reasons, including assistance to developing countries. More recently, the motivation in some countries has been more concerned with increasing revenues from the export of educational services, although policies towards overseas students generally serve multiple objectives. In general, financial motives have *supplemented* rather than *supplanted* cultural factors in driving student mobility.

2.1 Student flows: patterns and growth

The number of foreign students enrolled in tertiary education in OECD countries has doubled over the past 20 years.[2] In the late 1990s, foreign enrolments were growing nearly twice as fast as domestic ones (by 9% and 5%, respectively, from 1995 to 1999). By 1999, there were about 1.5 million foreign students in OECD countries – although at some 4% this is still only a small minority of all tertiary students. However, there are huge differences among countries, both in terms of volume and growth. In Australia, around one in seven university students is now from overseas. In the United Kingdom foreign enrolments grew by a third from 1995 to 1999.

Where foreign students enrol

Over three-quarters of all foreign students in OECD countries are in six countries: the United States (with 31% of all enrolments in 1999), the United Kingdom (15%), Germany (12%), France (9%), Australia (7%) and Japan (4%) (see Figure 4.1 overleaf). But the trends among these and other countries have been markedly different. As shown in Figure 4.2, the 1990s saw foreign student numbers

---

2. Unless otherwise indicated, data in this chapter from 1995 onwards are derived from the OECD Education Database and the annual OECD publication *Education at a Glance*; data prior to 1995 and for non-OECD countries are derived from the UNESCO *Statistical Yearbook*. Those publications detail the definitions and methodologies used. There are problems of international comparability with the data on foreign students. As noted in *Education at a Glance*, countries differ in the extent to which they include students who have entered a country to pursue education, as well as non-citizens who are in the country as the result of prior immigration. The OECD is working with Member countries to develop more relevant and comparable data on foreign students.

THE GROWTH OF CROSS-BORDER EDUCATION

Figure 4.1 Number of foreign tertiary students in OECD countries, by host country, 1999

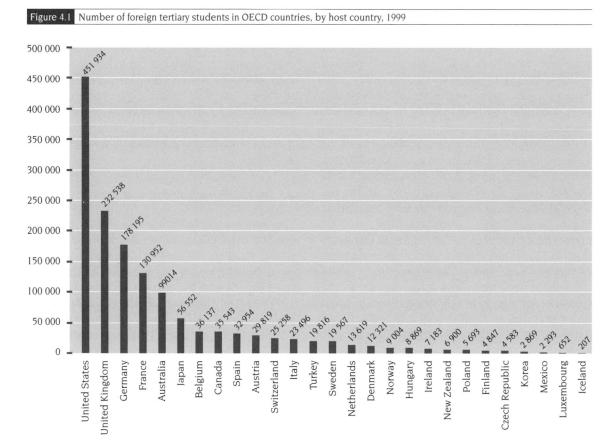

Note: Apart from Canada, Korea, Turkey and the United Kingdom for which the data refer only to non-resident international students who came to those countries to study, the other countries' data include both resident and non-resident foreign tertiary students (ISCED 5A, 5B and 6). Thus, the number of overseas students is generally overestimated, especially in countries like Germany and Switzerland where the access of foreigners to citizenship is (or was) limited. For example, 34% of foreign students in Germany were resident foreigners in 1999. In 1999, 50% of foreign students in Switzerland and Sweden were resident foreigners. However, the data for New Zealand exclude most Australian students, and are thus underestimated. In the United Kingdom, foreign students are defined by home address, so that even the number of non-resident international students might be underestimated.

Source: OECD Education database.

---

more than triple in Australia, almost triple in the United Kingdom, more than double in New Zealand, and grow substantially in Austria, Germany and Japan, while remaining relatively stable in Canada, France and the United States.

These changes are altering the relative position of countries as destinations for overseas students. France fell from second to fourth position as a receiving country between 1980 and 1999. There has been some reduction in the concentration of students in a few large countries: the share of the eight biggest receiving countries fell by 5% between 1995 and 1999. Although the four largest English-speaking countries (the United States, the United Kingdom, Canada and Australia) continue to take over half of all foreign students (54%),

clearly benefiting from the importance of English as the main language of international business, their overall share did not increase in the late 1990s. The relative shares of the United States and Canada declined, while those of the United Kingdom, Australia, New Zealand and Ireland grew or remained stable.

The courses most popular with foreign students

Although most foreign tertiary students are enrolled in undergraduate courses, compared with domestic students a higher proportion generally enrol at postgraduate level. In the United Kingdom for example, whereas only 9% of British higher education students are enrolled at postgraduate level, 26% of students from EU countries, and

---

Figure 4.2 Increase of foreign tertiary students in OECD countries, 1980-1999 (1990 = 100)

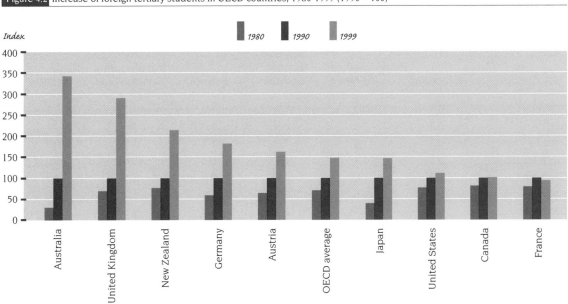

Note: "Foreign students" are defined in the note to Figure 4.1. The "OECD average" is the mean average of all OECD countries for which data are available for the years concerned. The countries shown are those which enrol substantial numbers of overseas students and which have data for the three years. Data for Germany do not include the former East Germany in 1980 and 1990, but 1999 data include the former East Germany, which accounts for part of the apparent enrolment growth since 1980.

The ISCED classification on educational levels was changed in 1997, so that data from before and after 1997 are not fully comparable. Tertiary education corresponds to ISCED levels 5A, 5B, 6 in the new classification, which might not cover exactly the same programmes as ISCED 5, 6 and 7 in the former classification; see *www.uis.unesco.org/en/act/act_p/isced.html* for details.

Source: UNESCO for 1980 and 1990, except for Japan (Ministry of Education); OECD for 1999. ....

Data for Figure 4.2, p. 115.

41% of students from other overseas countries, are in postgraduate courses. In the United States, about 45% of international students are enrolled at postgraduate level, compared with 17% of higher education students overall.

Overseas students also differ somewhat from domestic students in the fields that they study. In the English-speaking countries in particular, higher proportions of overseas students enrol in engineering, social sciences, business and law than do students overall (see Table 4.2 overleaf). In the United States, for example, 20% of all foreign students study Business and Management and 15% study Engineering. In all the countries shown in Table 4.2, smaller proportions of overseas students than domestic students are enrolled in Education. In general, slightly lower proportions of overseas students are enrolled in Health and Welfare (except in Poland, Hungary, the Czech Republic and Italy), and slightly higher proportions in Humanities and Arts.

Where foreign students come from

To understand these trends, it helps to look also at where foreign students are coming from. The majority of foreign students in OECD countries originate from outside the OECD area – about 57%. The OECD is a net "exporter" of educational services to developing countries, and hosts about 85% of all foreign students worldwide. Only one non-OECD member country, the Russian Federation, which is the sixth largest in terms of enrolments, is among the top ten receiving countries.[3]

However, the pattern of origin among foreign students in various OECD countries differs considerably. Most notably, as shown in Table 4.3 overleaf, the English-speaking countries have a particularly large share of students from Asia: three-quarters in all. Asians represent the biggest group of foreign students in

---

3. There are no data available on the number of foreign students studying in China.

Table 4.2 International tertiary students' field of study compared with all students, 2000

Index numbers: value 1.0 indicates equal % of international and all students – see note

	Education	Humanities and Arts	Social Sciences, Business, and Law	Science	Engineering, Manufacturing Construction	Health and Welfare
Australia	0.3	0.5	1.5	1.0	1.2	0.7
Austria	0.5	2.0	0.8	1.0	1.0	1.1
Canada	0.3	1.0	1.0	1.4	1.7	0.9
Czech Republic	0.1	1.4	1.1	0.8	0.6	5.0
Denmark	0.3	1.0	0.9	0.8	1.5	1.3
Finland	0.5	1.6	0.9	1.0	1.0	0.8
Germany	0.6	1.3	1.0	0.9	1.2	0.8
Hungary	0.5	1.5	0.4	0.5	1.0	3.7
Iceland	0.4	3.7	0.5	1.0	0.3	0.5
Italy	0.6	1.0	0.6	0.8	0.8	3.2
Japan	0.7	1.2	0.9	0.7	0.9	1.2
Netherlands	0.6	1.5	1.1	1.2	1.3	0.9
Norway	0.5	1.4	0.9	1.4	1.0	0.8
New Zealand	0.4	0.6	1.7	0.9	1.1	0.6
Poland	0.7	2.3	0.8	0.5	0.6	9.1
Sweden	0.5	1.2	1.1	1.2	1.0	1.1
Switzerland	0.5	1.2	1.0	1.3	1.1	0.6
United Kingdom	0.5	1.0	1.3	0.8	1.7	0.5

Note: The figures are an index of the extent to which the percentage of international students in a field of study is the same as the percentage for all students in the same field. An index of 1.0 means that the percentage of international students who study a particular field is the same as the percentage of all students studying that field. An index greater than 1.0 indicates that international students study in that field to a greater extent than do students overall.

Source: OECD Education database.

Table 4.3 English-speaking countries' shares of foreign tertiary students by origin, 1995 and 1999 (%)

	United States		United Kingdom		Australia		Canada		New Zealand		Ireland		Total of the 6 countries	
Origin of students	1995	1999	1995	1999	1995	1999	1995	1999	1995	1999	1995	1999	1995	1999
Asia/Oceania	49	44	7	11	12	13	5	2	1	1	0	0	74	73
Americas	56	49	9	15	1	3	6	5	0.2	0.3	1	1	72	71
Europe	19	14	17	24	1	1	2	2	0.1	0.1	1	1	39	41
European Union	16	12	20	28	1	1	5	2	0.1	0.1	1	1	42	44
OECD countries	35	31	12	14	6	7	4	2	0.5	0.5	0.4	0.5	58	56

Note: The table shows that 49% of the foreign students coming from the Asia/Oceania region in 1995 were studying in the United States, and 74% of the students from this region were studying in the six English-speaking countries concerned in 1995.

Source: OECD Education database.

OECD countries, with 45% of the total in 1999, of which 9% came from China (including Hong Kong, China), the biggest single country of origin. Economic growth has fuelled demand from Asian countries, where domestic systems have not grown fast enough to meet demand, and where students and their families often pay a high proportion of education costs, so studying abroad is not always much more expensive. However, the proportion of OECD foreign students from Asian countries fell slightly in the late 1990s (by two percentage points), reflecting the effects of the financial crisis in the region. In contrast, the number of European students studying abroad rose faster than in other regions, and the share of Europeans increased by four percentage points. Most European foreign students remained within Europe, with four in ten going to English-speaking countries. It must be borne in mind, however, that while this helps explain why English-speaking countries have not increased their *share* of foreign enrolments, both the number of Asian students studying abroad and the number of all foreign students enrolled in English-speaking countries continued to grow in *absolute* terms.

Regional concentrations

Do these trends also reflect a growing regionalisation of study patterns? A number of factors have led students from certain countries to study primarily in certain others, notably:

– *Geographical or cultural proximity.* English-speaking students go primarily to other English-speaking countries, and Scandinavian students mainly to Scandinavian ones. A large share of foreign students in France come from former French colonies, 40% from Africa. Nine in ten foreign students in Australia are from the Asia-Pacific region.

– *Bilateral agreements* between countries *or national policies* to foster student exchange mobility or fund specific international projects involving educational institutions. Public or private scholarship programmes partly fund domestic or foreign students' international studies in all OECD countries.

– *Larger-scale international programmes* fostering international mobility of post-secondary education on a regional basis, for example in the Asia-Pacific region, Europe and North America. The European Union's Socrates programme is perhaps the most ambitious of these, aiming to strengthen European citizenship and promote mobility in employment as well as education. Since 1987, Erasmus, the main post-secondary element of Socrates, has enabled approximately one million tertiary students to spend a study period abroad in another European Union or affiliated country. It has also developed a common European Credit Transfer System (ECTS) and funded teacher mobility.

Yet, as shown in Table 4.4, concentrations within regions vary greatly, and are changing in different ways. In 1999, 83% of European foreign students in OECD countries were studying in an OECD Member country located in Europe, and 55% of

---

Table 4.4 **Distribution of foreign students enrolled in OECD countries, by region, 1995 and 1999 (%)**

Origin of students	1995 OECD countries in				1999 OECD countries in			
	Europe	EU	Americas	Asia-Oceania	Europe	EU	Americas	Asia-Oceania
Europe	77	69	21	2	83	74	16	2
European Union	78	70	21	1	84	77	15	1
Americas	34	32	62	4	40	38	55	5
Asia-Oceania	25	23	54	21	30	28	47	23
OECD countries	50	46	39	11	54	49	34	12

Note: The table shows that 77% of European foreign students in OECD countries in 1995 were studying in OECD Member countries located in Europe, and 62% of foreign students from the Americas who were studying in OECD countries were studying in OECD Member countries located in America (*i.e.* the USA, Canada and Mexico).

Source: OECD Education database.

foreign students from the Americas who were studying in OECD countries were in an OECD country located in the Americas (*i.e.* the United States, Canada or Mexico). However, only 23% of the foreign students from Asia and Oceania who were studying in an OECD country were in an OECD Member country in that region (*i.e.* Australia, Japan, Korea or New Zealand).[4] Although the number of Asian students in Australia and New Zealand has been growing, most foreign students from this region continue to go to North America and Europe. Conversely, while OECD countries in Europe have increased their share of foreign students from the Americas, a greater number of

American students continue to go to the United States, Canada or Mexico. Among Europeans, intra-regional concentration increased between 1995 and 1999. Undoubtedly, the European Union's policies have been critical: the Erasmus programme funded 38% of EU students studying in other EU countries in 1999.

2.2 Student flows and the balance of trade

While governments and international bodies have long promoted student mobility mainly for cultural and educational reasons, it also serves to expand world trade in services, and the trade reasons

Figure 4.3 Number of foreign students per domestic student abroad in tertiary education by OECD country, 1995 and 1999

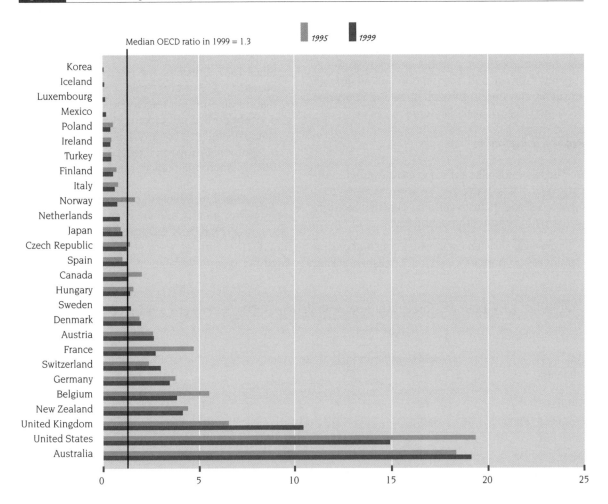

Note: "Foreign students" are defined in the note to Figure 4.1. The "median OECD" figure indicates that in 1999 half of the OECD countries had a ratio of more than 1.3. In 1999, the mean average ratio for OECD countries was 2.8.

Source: OECD Education database. ....

Data for Figure 4.3, p. 115.

Table 4.5 **Export earnings from foreign students and as a percentage of total export earnings from services, 1989, 1997 and 2000**

	1989		1997		2000	
	US$ million	% of total service exports	US$ million	% of total service exports	US$ million	% of total service exports
Australia	584	6.6	2 190	11.8	2 155	11.8
Canada	530	3.0	595	1.9	796	2.1
Mexico	..	..	52	0.5	29	0.2
New Zealand	..	..	280	6.6	199	4.7
Poland	..	..	16	0.2	..	..
United Kingdom	2 214	4.5	4 080	4.3	3 758	3.2
United States	4 575	4.4	8 346	3.5	10 280	3.5
Greece	..	..	..	..	80	0.4
Italy	..	..	..	..	1 170	2.1

Note: The US$ figures are expressed in terms of current prices. The earnings figures are estimates based on samples of businesses and institutions, and are therefore subject to sampling error and the range of non-sampling errors involved in survey work. Australia, Italy and New Zealand include students from levels other than tertiary education in the trade in educational services data. For all other countries, the data correspond to tertiary students only.

Source: OECD statistics on trade in services; IMF data for Italy and the United States in 2000, and Poland for 1997; the Office for National Statistics for the United Kingdom in 1997 and 2000.

have become more prominent in recent years. For a country's economy, the enrolment of a foreign student represents an "invisible export" through the associated income flow. In terms of the student flows described above, the balance varies greatly from one country to another. Figure 4.3 shows for OECD countries the number of foreign students received per domestic student who is studying overseas: those with ratios greater than one are "net exporters" of educational services, while those with less than one are "net importers". On average, OECD countries in 1999 hosted 2.8 overseas students for every domestic student who was studying abroad. However, in only seven countries is the ratio higher than this, while 11 are net "importers": they enrol fewer foreign students than the number of nationals studying abroad. Given that the mean ratio is inflated by a few countries with a very high ratio (Australia, the United States and the United Kingdom), perhaps a better indicator of the pattern of student flows is provided by the median ratio, which was 1.3 in 1999.

Trade in educational services can also be expressed in terms of value, *i.e* the money spent by overseas students on fees, living costs and expenses. It was estimated to be worth a minimum of US$30 billion

in 1998, or about 3% of the total value of services exports (Larsen *et al.*, 2002). Increasing awareness of the significant size of the international market in educational services and of its growth potential partly explains the growing competition among nations and institutions to keep or extend market share.

As shown in Table 4.5, during the 1990s export earnings from foreign students increased sharply in the countries for which data are available. Since students travelling to and studying in foreign countries represent the largest element of cross-border trade in educational services, this indicator is often used to estimate the overall level of trade in such services. However, the rapid growth of other forms of educational trade will make it a less satisfactory proxy as time goes on.

Note that in most of the countries shown, rapid growth in the value of educational service exports has been paralleled by growth in export earnings

4. Note that these data include countries of origin but not countries of study outside the OECD area. Thus they may underestimate the concentration of Asians studying within all Asian countries: about 70% of foreign students in Malaysia and India, for example, are of Asian origin.

from services overall, so the share of education in total services exports has fallen over the 1990s in most countries for which data are available. The sole exception is Australia, where the export value of educational services almost quadrupled between 1989 and 2000, and the share of education in total service exports almost doubled to 11.8%. In Australia, education has become the third largest export earner in services (and the 14th largest export earner overall). Education has also become an important export earner for New Zealand, accounting for almost 5% of service export earnings in 2000 as the fourth largest export earner in services (and the 15th largest overall).

Table 4.6 shows data on the "import" of educational services, in terms of payments made for or by domestic students studying abroad. Australia, Greece and Italy are the largest importers of educational services expressed as a percentage of total service imports among the OECD countries for which data are available. It is noteworthy that in absolute terms, the United States is both the biggest importer and the biggest exporter of the countries for which data are available, and two other major exporters of educational services – Australia and Canada – also make substantial payments to overseas suppliers of education. Trade in educational services, as with much of trade in other goods and services, is not necessarily in only one direction.

2.3 Supply-side efforts to boost trade

In some countries, governments and institutions have taken explicit initiatives to boost the value of foreign student trade, for example through marketing initiatives and the setting of fees for foreign students that are different from those charged to domestic ones. These strategies include the funding of bodies to advertise national higher education in international fairs and to welcome and help foreign students (see Box 4.1).

It must be borne in mind that trade is only one of several reasons for wanting to attract overseas students; others include enriching the educational experiences of domestic students, and building long-term ties between nations. One indicator of the importance attached to the revenue-raising motive is the level of tuition fees charged to foreign students as compared with that charged to domestic students. As shown in Table 4.7, these vary considerably from one country to another. Countries that charge higher tuition fees for foreign students include Australia and New Zealand, where guidelines require universities to charge at least the full cost for foreign students, and Canada and the United Kingdom, where universities are allowed to set their own rates.

However, the divisions are not only between domestic and foreign students: state universities

Table 4.6 Import payments by national students studying abroad and as a percentage of total import payments for services, 1989, 1997 and 2000

	1989		1997		2000	
	US$ million	% of total service imports	US$ million	% of total service imports	US$ million	% of total service imports
Australia	178	1.3	410	2.2	356	2.0
Canada	258	1.1	532	1.4	602	1.4
Mexico	..	..	44	0.3	53	0.3
Poland	..	..	41	0.7	..	..
United Kingdom	67	0.2	182	0.2	150	0.2
United States	586	0.7	1396	0.9	2150	1.0
Greece	..	..	..	..	211	1.9
Italy	..	..	..	..	849	1.5

Note and source: see Table 4.5.

> ## Box 4.1 Examples of initiatives to attract international students
>
> *Australia*: Several bodies promote Australian educational services abroad: the most important are the governmental organisations Australian Education International and Austrade, and the private organisation IDP Education Australia.
>
> *United Kingdom*: In 1999, the United Kingdom government set an objective of 75 000 more overseas students by 2005. While the British Council was granted US$8.2 million for the international promotion of higher education in the United Kingdom, the Education Counselling Service spends US$1.6 million for its promotion campaigns in South America, China, India, Russia and Israel.
>
> *France*: In 1998, the Ministries of Education and Foreign Affairs launched the Edufrance Agency to set up and implement a marketing and communication strategy directed at foreign students with a budget of US$16 million over four years. Its target was to double the number of foreign students in France over the four-year period. It should be noted, however, that almost all foreign students pay the same low tuition fees as French students.
>
> *Other examples*: The Canadian Bureau for International Education and the Canadian Education Centre Network in Canada, Education New Zealand in New Zealand, the Institute of International Education in the United States, and the DAAD (*Deutscher Akademischer Austauschdienst*) in Germany.

in the United States favour local students, and out-of-state and foreign students are charged higher fees; Australia and New Zealand exempt each other's students from overseas rates. A number of EU countries charge no fees to any students, while others such as Austria, Switzerland or the Slovak Republic charge higher tuition fees for international students (albeit with a number of exemptions for particular students) but, compared with some other OECD countries, make limited efforts to attract foreign students. Although domestic and international students pay low or no tuition fees

in Germany, two *Länder* (Baden Wurtemberg and Berlin) have recently introduced tuition fees for higher education that will apply to international as well as domestic students. In France, international students pay the same low fee as domestic students, but the EduFrance agency charges fees for new (optional) additional language training and tutoring.

National policies on tuition fees for post-secondary study can also affect a domestic student's decision about whether to study at home or go abroad. As

Table 4.7 Level of tuition fees in public universities for international students compared to domestic students

Tuition fee structure	Countries
Higher tuition fees for international students than domestic students	Australia, Austria*, Belgium,* Canada, Ireland*, New Zealand, Slovak Republic, Switzerland*, United Kingdom*, United States
Same tuition fees for international and domestic students	France, Greece, Hungary, Iceland, Italy, Japan, Korea, Netherlands, Portugal, Spain
No tuition fees for either international or domestic students	Czech Republic, Denmark, Finland, Germany, Norway, Poland, Sweden

* For non-European Union or European Economic Area students.
Source: Eurydice; European Society for Engineering Education (SEFI); OECD. ....

Figure 4.4 Percentage of direct expenditure for tertiary educational institutions coming from students' households, 1998

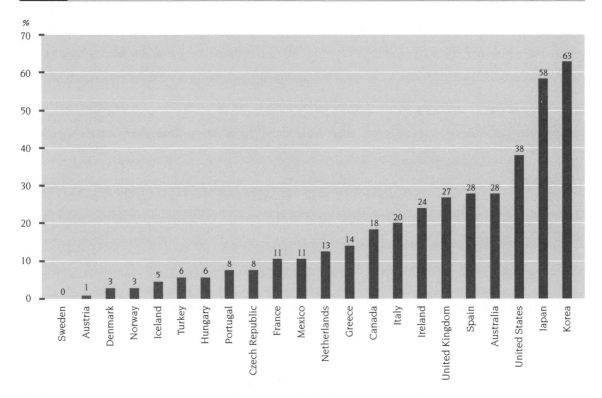

Note: The indicator expresses direct expenditure for tertiary educational institutions coming privately from households as a percentage of direct expenditure from all sources for tertiary educational institutions.

Source: OECD Education database. ....

Figure 4.4 shows, OECD countries differ markedly in the extent to which students contribute to the direct costs of providing higher education. The proportions range from less than 5% of direct costs in some of the Nordic countries[5] to well over 50% in Japan and Korea. This may help to explain why Japanese and Korean students make up relatively high proportions of the foreign students studying in other OECD countries. Yet, since many of them go to study in the United States, where students also pay a relatively high proportion of the direct costs of higher education, it is clear that international student mobility is influenced by a wider range of factors than tuition fees alone.

2.4 Influences on student demand

In general, the countries that attract the most foreign students (Figure 4.1) charge the highest tuition fees (Table 4.7). In part, this reflects the fact that educational institutions have a strong

incentive to attract overseas students where they generate substantial revenues.[6] This has certainly been an important factor in the growth of overseas student numbers in Australia (although some overseas students are also subsidised by the government). Still, students will not continue to pay high fees unless they perceive they are getting value for money. Students' decisions about undertaking study in another country involve

5. Norway and Denmark also often contribute substantially to the costs incurred by their students studying abroad. In Norway, domestic students are funded through grants and loans that they can use to study in any country and institution they wish. In Denmark, domestic students can obtain grants and loans for study abroad for up to four years under certain conditions. These policies help to explain the relatively high enrolment rates abroad of Norwegian and Danish students.

6. A policy of charging foreign students more than domestic students can also reflect a desire not to cross-subsidise foreign students from domestic students' fees.

balancing the costs of study against the expected benefits, both monetary and non-monetary, arising from study overseas compared with study in their home country.

Students today have many reasons for wanting to study overseas, including both broader opportunities in terms of perceived quality and coverage of courses compared to their home country and the advantage of having a better understanding of the world beyond their home country. Their decisions are influenced by a wide array of factors that need to be considered by institutions or countries wanting to boost the number of overseas students. They include:

– The accessibility and variety of post-secondary studies in the home country (*e.g.* restricted quotas on some courses);

– The language of the host country and in which courses are provided (English-speaking countries generally have a competitive advantage in this area, although some non English-speaking countries are now offering courses in English to attract foreign students);

– The geographical and cultural proximity between the host and home countries, as well as historical links;

– The availability of support networks, including past and present students from the home country;

– The reputation and perceived quality of educational institutions or of education as a whole in the host country in relation to education in the home country;

– The transferability and/or recognition of qualifications between the home country and the receiving country;

– The cost of study abroad compared to the cost of study at home, including tuition fees, costs of living, and the availability of different forms of financial support;

– The infrastructure and social benefits for foreign students in the host country (*e.g.* health cover, accommodation, language centres, right to social security);

– The immigration (or visa) policy towards students, and especially the possibility for overseas students to work while studying and to stay in the country after their studies; and

– Labour market opportunities in the host and home countries.

3. NEW FORMS OF TRADE IN EDUCATIONAL SERVICES

Although study abroad is presently the largest component of international trade in post-secondary education, two other forms are growing in importance: distance learning (Mode 1 in Table 4.1) and commercial presence (Mode 3). Distance learning includes e-learning courses via the Internet and other communication means (satellite, TV, CD-ROM, mail). Examples of commercial presence include branches of universities operating abroad to meet the demand from students who do not wish or are unable to study overseas, language training companies, and other education or training companies from both the public and private sectors. Such forms of provision may also include students spending part of their study in the host country (Mode 2) and staff from the exporting country spending time teaching in the students' home country (Mode 4).

Offshore campuses and distance learning are often attractive to students because they involve lower costs than studying abroad. Although they may not enrich students with the same cultural and linguistic experiences as foreign study, they are likely to meet a growing demand in the future. Such forms of provision raise important policy questions for national governments because they expand domestic students' opportunities and provide direct competition to local education providers.

Australia is a striking example of a country whose exports of post-secondary educational services are increasingly delivered in the students' home country: between 1996 and 2001, such "offshore" enrolments increased from 24% to 37% of all international students enrolled in Australian institutions (see Figure 4.5 overleaf). Most of these students attended offshore campuses (28% of all

THE GROWTH OF CROSS-BORDER EDUCATION

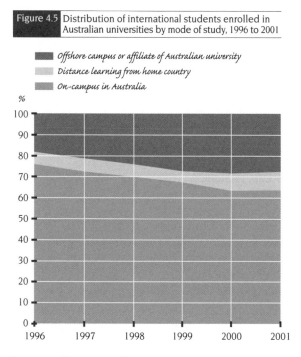

Figure 4.5 Distribution of international students enrolled in Australian universities by mode of study, 1996 to 2001

■ Offshore campus or affiliate of Australian university
■ Distance learning from home country
■ On-campus in Australia

Source: IDP Education Australia.
Data for Figure 4.5, p. 115.

international students in 2001) and relatively few (9% of all international students) were enrolled offshore in distance education, although the number doing so is growing. More than half of the international students from Singapore and Hong Kong, China studying in an Australian educational institution are enrolled in offshore courses.[7]

The United Kingdom is another major provider of courses overseas, with trade expanding rapidly in this area during the 1990s. In 1996-97, there were around 140 000 students enrolled in British institutions overseas, compared with around 200 000 international students in the United Kingdom the same year (Bennell and Pearce, 1998). In Hong Kong, China, the United Kingdom accounted for over half of the 575 foreign degrees offered through local private colleges, distance education centres or in partnership with local universities in 2000. One-third of such degrees were offered by Australian institutions, with the rest coming from other countries including the United States and mainland China (McBurnie and Ziguras, 2001).

Growth in new modes of international delivery of education has been stimulated partly by the

emergence of new types of providers. Although few statistical data are currently available, this is one of the most important features of the changing environment of international education and training (Cunningham *et al.*, 2000). These new providers include, in particular, corporate training institutions, for-profit institutions, and distance learning (including e-learning) institutions.

These new institutions compete with traditional post-secondary institutions, but there is no sharp dichotomy between the old and the new. Traditional institutions are part of the changing picture, sometimes creating private arms or virtual branches, or entering into partnerships with other institutions such as private media companies.

Corporate training institutions are generally spin-offs of multinational companies, which mostly train their employees across the world but also train other learners, suppliers and customers. According to a recent survey of US "corporate universities", such as those operated by Motorola or McDonald's, 42% provide courses for which a degree could be granted at an accredited educational institution (Densford, 1999). Around a quarter attract revenue from outside the corporation (Meister, 1998). The number of North American corporate universities quadrupled from 400 in 1988 to over 1 600 in 1998, and many of these have multiple campuses or branches. For example, Microsoft's 1 700 Certified Technical Education Centers (CTECs) are franchised private training companies operating internationally, using Microsoft-certified trainers and the Microsoft curriculum. Microsoft also licenses its curriculum to educational institutions across the world. For example, around 40 universities and colleges in the United Kingdom have a contract to teach Microsoft-certified classes. Such courses are often very attractive to potential students because they provide stronger recognition and job opportunities than do some qualifications from traditional universities.

Although they have existed for over a century, *for-profit universities* are growing in importance, and are increasingly involved in education across national borders. Sylvan Learning Systems is

---

7. IDP Education Australia. Cf. *www.idp.edu.au/services/marketing/ research_consult/fast_facts/higher_education.asp.*

one of the most striking examples. The company includes brand names such as Sylvan Learning Centers, Caliber Learning Networks and Wall Street Institutes. Sylvan has recently bought private universities and business schools in Mexico, Spain, Chile, France and Switzerland. It also owns a majority stake in a leading graduate distance learning institution, Walden University, and the National Technology University, a distance learning provider of engineering courses and degrees. Those institutions provide courses and qualifications on a fee-for-service basis to domestic and international students, workers and companies. In 2001, the Sylvan group reported a 54% rise in revenue to US$485 million.

Information and communication technology (ICT) facilitates the offshore delivery of educational services by complementing traditional face-to-face education with interactive ways of learning and of disseminating material (e-mails, videoconferences, and so on). Widely used as a complement to conventional face-to-face teaching in post-secondary institutions, the market for virtual education institutions has followed the ups and downs of the e-economy. However, virtual education institutions, which teach predominantly via ICT, are still regarded as having a high growth potential, especially in the markets for corporate training and education for adults. For example, the National Technology University offers 15 Master's degree programmes online and provides access to four other University Master's degrees. The Internet education company Unext and its Cardean University deliver business courses to companies as well as to individual students, relying on a consortium of elite American and British universities. Cardean University has recently signed an agreement with Thomson Enterprise Learning to market on-line business education programmes to major corporate clients worldwide.

In order to meet the competition of for-profit and virtual universities, some *traditional universities* have created for-profit arms targeting e-learning demands as well as adult education. In 2002, the University of Liverpool (United Kingdom) and the Washington University of Saint Louis (United States) both launched MBAs in China: the British university adopted a fully online model whereas its American counterpart sent in academic staff to work with a partner Chinese university. A grow-

ing number of traditional universities are also creating consortia and partnerships designed to address international demand through new modes of delivery. For example, Universitas 21 brings together 18 established universities from ten countries to pursue global initiatives that would be beyond their individual capabilities. In partnership with Thomson Learning, Universitas 21 has created U21global, an online (and television) provider, scheduled to deliver business courses from 2003 in Singapore, Malaysia and Hong Kong, China. Trium EMBA is another example of an international partnership, in this case involving United States, United Kingdom and French universities delivering Executive MBAs through a mix of face-to-face teaching and distance learning.

4. TRADE IN EDUCATION AND THE GATS

As noted earlier, greater international trade in educational services is being driven by new forms of supply and increased demand from students. The issue of trade liberalisation in educational services has been put firmly on the agenda through its inclusion in the ongoing negotiations of the General Agreement on Trade in Services (GATS). In practice, however, this liberalisation raises much public debate and countries have proven highly sensitive about subjecting education to free trade so far.

The GATS is a multilateral, legally enforceable agreement governing international trade in services. It offers for trade in services mutually agreed rules, binding market access and non-discriminatory commitments in the same way that the General Agreement on Tariffs and Trade (GATT) does for trade in goods. The GATS, which entered into force in 1995, is administered by the World Trade Organization (WTO) and its advent reflects the growing importance of services in international trade.

Table 4.8 overleaf outlines the key elements and rules of the GATS, which consists of three core components: the framework of rules that lays out general obligations; annexes on specific service sectors; and the schedules of commitments submitted by each member country, detailing liberalisation undertakings by sector and mode of supply. Negotiations under the GATS resumed in 2000.

Table 4.8 **GATS obligations and rules**		
GATS element or rule	**Explanation**	**Application**
Scope and coverage	All internationally traded services are covered in the 12 different service sectors. (*e.g.* education, transportation, financial, tourism, health, construction)	Applies to all services – with two exceptions: i) services provided in the exercise of governmental authority; ii) air traffic rights
Measures	All laws, regulations and practices at the national or sub-national levels affecting trade in services	Measures taken by central, regional or local governments and authorities and non-governmental bodies in the exercise of powers delegated by central, regional and local governments and authorities
General obligations	Three general obligations exist in GATS – most favoured nation treatment (MFN) – transparency – dispute settlement	They apply to all service sectors regardless of whether WTO members schedule commitments or not
Most favoured nation (MFN) treatment	Requires equal and consistent treatment of all foreign trading partners MFN means treating one's trading partners equally. Under GATS, if a country allows foreign competition in a sector, equal opportunities in that sector should be given to service providers from all WTO members	One-time exemptions are permissible for original WTO signatories and newly acceding countries, but they should not *in principle* exceed a period of 10 years. In any event, they shall be subject to negotiation in subsequent trade liberalisation rounds
Sector-specific obligations	There are a number of sector-specific obligations attached to national schedules, among which are market access and national treatment	Only applies to commitments listed in national schedules Degree and extent of obligation is determined by country; countries retain the right to maintain non-conforming measures in scheduled sectors and modes of supply
National treatment	Aims for equal treatment for foreign and domestic providers (or equal competitive opportunities where identical treatment is not possible) Once a foreign supplier has been allowed to supply a service in one's country, there should be no discrimination in treatment between the foreign and domestic providers	Only applies where a country has made a positive specific commitment Non-conforming measures can be retained negatively in scheduled sectors/modes of supply
Market access	Primary focus on non-discriminatory quantitative restrictions impeding access to markets	Each country determines limitations on market access for each committed sector and mode of supply, as per national treatment
Progressive liberalisation	GATS has a built-in agenda which means that negotiations can be re-examined periodically with a view to achieving a progressively higher level of bound liberalisation; special flexibility is envisaged for developing countries in this regard	Each country determines the pace, extent and nature of market opening under GATS and retains the right to schedule no commitments in any sector/mode of supply

Source: OECD.

Education is one of the sectors for which WTO Members have been least inclined to make commitments. To date, 25 OECD countries and 28 other WTO members have made commitments for at least one education sub-sector:[8] primary education including pre-school services; secondary education; higher education including university and post-secondary vocational services; adult education; or other education. On the whole, they have maintained slightly more limitations on primary than on secondary, higher or adult education, and have been more sensitive about foreign institutions, companies and professionals operating in their countries (Modes 3 and 4) than about cross-border supply (Mode 1) or students travelling abroad (Mode 2).

4.1 Public educational services and the GATS

The GATS exempts services "supplied in the exercise of governmental authority", which includes "any [service] which is supplied neither on a commercial basis, nor in competition with one or more service suppliers". Since in many countries public educational services do compete to some extent with private ones, it can be argued that this exemption does not apply. However, this may turn on whether the public and private providers are supplying "like services". Moreover, charging fees does not automatically make public provision "commercial".

Whatever the interpretation of this rule, some countries have proposed further liberalisation of trade in educational services in the present GATS negotiations. Their proposals recall that the GATS terms are consistent with governments' right to regulate in order to meet domestic policy objectives within the education sector.[9] Three of the four detailed proposals that have been put forward to date (from Australia, New Zealand and the United States) stress the rapid expansion of higher education and adult education and training, particularly through the use of the Internet, and their increasing international significance. Australia, in particular, argues for the further liberalisation of trade in educational services primarily as a means of providing individuals in all countries with access to a wide range of options. The fourth negotiating proposal, from Japan, encourages WTO members "to promote liberalisation in the educational services sector

through better market access, further assurance of national treatment and deregulation of related domestic regulations". However, the Japanese proposal also stresses the need to establish measures to maintain and improve the quality of the services through protection of consumers from low-quality education providers operating across borders, and ensuring the international equivalence of qualifications (see Section 5 below).

4.2 Foreign education providers and public subsidies

The GATS is a very flexible negotiating framework. WTO members retain the freedom to choose not only the sectors and modes of supply for which they want to make market access and national treatment commitments, but also to determine the content of those commitments and the scope of any retained restrictions.

Even if a country has made a commitment which implies that there is a requirement to treat foreign and domestic education suppliers equally, any WTO member wishing to treat foreign providers of (say) university courses less favourably than domestic providers can do so, provided this is specified in its schedule of commitments. For example, the European Union, which is negotiating on behalf of its Member states, takes the general position that the national treatment "rule" does not apply to the provision of subsidies to foreign providers within public education: governments are not required to provide them with subsidies on the same conditions as domestic providers. Similarly, the United States has a national treatment limitation regarding access to certain grants and scholarships.

4.3 The GATS and recognition of qualifications

Member countries are required to notify the WTO whenever they enter into bilateral or multilateral agreements concerning education or experience obtained, requirements met, or licences or certifica-

---

8. For a more detailed overview of country commitments at WTO, in the education services field, see OECD (2002c).

9. United States proposal on "Higher (post-secondary) Education, Adult Education and Training" to the current GATS negotiations (S/CSS/W/23), 18 December 2000.

tion granted in a particular country. The purpose is to provide other interested WTO countries with the opportunity to negotiate comparable recognition with the country concerned. The GATS also states that "wherever appropriate, recognition should be based on multilaterally agreed criteria. In appropriate cases, Members shall work in co-operation with relevant intergovernmental and non-governmental organisations towards the establishment and adoption of common international standards and criteria for recognition and common international standards for the practice of relevant services trades and professions". This requirement provides an opportunity for other countries to indicate their interest in joining the negotiations but it does not compel the original negotiating countries to accept others.

Accreditation, licensing and recognition procedures are largely domestic processes that often differ significantly between national systems, which can give rise to problems of transnational recognition.

Where government statutes or regulations require certification or accreditation by non-governmental organisations for the purpose of licensing, or where such authority is delegated, these are considered "measures of Members", and are therefore subject to provisions of the GATS agreement (Ascher, 2002).

4.4 Implications of the GATS for education

WTO members have agreed that the new trade liberalisation round should be finalised by 1 January 2005. The schedule is as follows:

- 30 June 2002: Countries file initial proposals asking trading partners to open their markets in service areas. Four negotiating proposals from Australia, Japan, New Zealand and the United States have been presented in educational services.

- 31 March 2003: Countries will present initial offers to open their markets in service areas.

- 1 January 2005: The present GATS negotiation round will end.

It is hard to assess accurately the implications of the GATS for the further liberalisation of interna-

tional trade in post-secondary education, since it will interact with the demand and supply trends identified in the previous sections, as well as with the many bilateral and regional trade agreements signed between countries with respect to educational services. The demand and supply trends include: the pace of increase in student demand, both in developed and developing countries; the need for higher education institutions to seek alternative sources of funding, which sometimes means engaging in for-profit activities or seeking private sector sources of financial support; rising tuition fees and other costs faced by students; and the growing number of private enterprises providing higher education and adult training, both domestically and internationally.

Many of these developments pre-date the GATS commitments in educational services, initiated in 1995 and have, if anything, accelerated since, despite the relatively low level of liberalisation commitments achieved in education under the GATS. More significantly, much of the trade in educational services takes place outside the WTO framework and is not reflected in GATS commitments (nor in regional trade agreements, for the most part). In this connection, it is worth noting that only a few of the countries that have substantial numbers of students studying overseas – China, Germany, France, Greece and Thailand – have made commitments in educational services to date. Furthermore, the GATS negotiations tend to concentrate on higher education and adult education and training, and not on primary and secondary education, which most countries are treating as off-limits with respect to liberalisation commitments.

Most countries are mainly interested in Mode 2 trade (students studying abroad). Few "trade barriers" impede such flows. The most important barriers are difficulties in obtaining student visas, funding study abroad, and dealing with student-related work permits. However, these issues cannot be addressed by the GATS negotiations (Sauvé, 2002). As well, Mode 4 trade in educational services (where someone travels to another country on a temporary basis to supply education) is not generally perceived as a major concern given the benefits that researchers and academics bring to the host country and its educational institutions.

Yet, even if the implications of the GATS for education have so far been very limited, some factors might change this picture in the longer term:

– Trade in educational services will most likely grow given the rise in foreign investment in off-shore activities (Mode 3 – commercial presence) and the increasing use of ICT as a means of delivering education (Mode 1 – cross-border supply). Ongoing WTO talks on educational services and electronic commerce might over time contribute to reducing the barriers to such trade.

– The GATS has an "in-built agenda", in which there are successive rounds of negotiations with a view to achieving progressively higher levels of trade liberalisation. This implies that the negotiations on trade in services at the WTO will continuously address the issue of how the international market in educational services can be further liberalised and the barriers to such trade removed or reduced.

5. INTERNATIONAL QUALITY ASSURANCE AND ACCREDITATION

Quality assurance and accreditation systems in post-secondary education are almost exclusively developed by the state and post-secondary institutions. In most cases, their focus is confined to assuring the quality of the programmes delivered in the country itself to domestic students. There is thus a general lack of transparency in the international education market in the sense that students sometimes have difficulties in assessing whether a course offered by a foreign education provider is of good quality or not. Furthermore, it is often not self-evident for students studying abroad that their qualifications will automatically be recognised in their home country. This puts the issue of international quality assurance and accreditation high on the policy agenda.

5.1 Divergence or convergence of international quality assurance and accreditation?

National quality assurance systems are highly relevant to international trade in educational services. If they are sufficiently comparable across countries and inspire sufficient confidence, they can contribute significantly to consumer protec-tion and the regulation of transnational education trade.

There is, however, considerable diversity in quality assurance and accreditation mechanisms across countries in terms of: the definition of "quality" itself; the purpose and functions of quality assurance such as institutional improvement or external account-ability and transparency; and the methodologies used in quality assurance and accreditation (Van Damme, 2002). In the United States for example, the quality assurance system depends on a complex matrix of state licensing and certification boards, central state higher education systems, regional accreditation agencies, professional accreditation agencies, and the federal government.

The "unsolved" questions of consumer protection and recognition of qualifications have put pressure on national quality assurance arrangements in post-secondary education to increase dialogue and co-operation with players in other countries. As a result, there has been some limited international convergence in national quality assurance and accreditation systems. A prominent example is the pan-European Bologna Declaration with its goal of a common framework of higher education degrees in Europe and developing "a European dimension in quality assurance, with comparable criteria and methods". Another major initiative is the UNESCO/Council of Europe Lisbon Convention on the Recognition of Qualifications Concerning Higher Education in the European Region adopted in 1997. This Convention no longer follows the "formal" logic of strict "equivalence" of qualifica-tions based on the concepts of "recognition" and "accreditation". Instead, it is based on *co-operation* and *trust* between national systems. If a country ratifies the Convention, that country will be bound to recognise qualifications from other parties to the Convention as similar to the corresponding qualifications in its own system unless a substantial difference can be shown between the qualifications of the parties.

Closely linked to the Lisbon Convention is the recent adoption by UNESCO and the Council of Europe of a "Code of Good Practice in the Provision of Transnational Education". This code implies that quality assurance arrangements should follow transnational provision from the exporting country to the receiving country, a principle which means that quality assurance systems are implicitly exported to countries in which they do not have any legally recognised status.

Concerns about the quality of transnational higher education programmes have already led to some of the main education exporting countries – Australia, New Zealand, the United Kingdom and the United States – expanding their national quality assurance systems so that they also apply to their cross-border provision of higher education. Participation by institutions is often voluntary, although many universities and local partners do take part.

The main drivers behind the growing diversification of post-secondary education are the increasing provision of cross-border and distance-learning delivery, and new private for-profit providers. However, in general, outside the United States, existing quality assurance and accreditation frameworks have so far not been very adaptive in dealing with new private for-profit providers and distance-learning provision (Van Damme, 2002). Currently, most quality assurance agencies seem oriented to protecting the traditional concepts of academic quality. These traditional concepts may not always adapt easily to more diversified provision by a wider range of providers. One possible response could be to diversify national quality and accreditation systems to reflect greater diversity in education provision. However, this would be unlikely to result in greater transparency and international convergence. Another response would be to reconceptualise and simplify quality assurance mechanisms so that they are capable of addressing very different forms of post-secondary education and transnational provision. So far, however, there is very little evidence that major changes within national quality assurance regimes will be made in the foreseeable future to achieve international consistency.

5.2 Professional recognition

In some countries, professions such as law, medicine and engineering require additional examinations and training following university to gain a licence to practice. In contrast, university degrees in other countries are often automatically recognised as giving access to professional careers without further examination or training. In English-speaking countries, for example, there are often accrediting bodies linked to professional associations that assess whether a higher education programme – and thus a student graduating from that programme – meets the standards imposed by the profession.

The increasing international mobility of professionals has led to mutual and multilateral recognition agreements to address issues of professional recognition and equivalency across borders. The WTO agreements and regional trade agreements have stimulated these developments. The accountancy profession is one such example. In 1998, the WTO adopted a regulation under which countries that have made trade commitments in accountancy services agreed to secure procedural transparency in licensing and qualifications. The regulation does not, however, focus on the *substantive content* of qualifications in accountancy. The WTO is not a standards-making body, nor is it mandated to assess the content of national standards, be they educational or professional. The role of WTO is foremost to guarantee transparency in recognition and licensing arrangements (see also Section 4.3 above).

One of the most far-reaching international agreements on mutual recognition of professional qualifications is the "Washington Accord" for the engineering profession, reached in 1997 between engineering organisations from Australia, Canada, Ireland, New Zealand, the United Kingdom and the United States. South Africa and Hong Kong, China have recently joined, and Japan has provisional membership. The Accord recognises the "substantial equivalence" of each other's programmes in satisfying the academic requirements for the practice of engineering, while not yet formally mutually recognising professional qualifications. The Accord also includes criteria and procedures for the accreditation of academic engineering programmes. The signatories accept accreditation decisions among each other and thus recognise the equivalency of the national accreditation mechanisms in each country.

The ICT industries are particularly active in worldwide licensing measures for corporate ICT education and training programmes. A key actor in this area is CompTIA, which represents more than 8 000 computing and communication companies in several countries and provides standards in certification. IBM, Intel, Microsoft and Novell have incorporated CompTIA certification in their own certification training. Such initiatives have an indirect influence on quality assurance and accreditation arrangements in vocational education and training and, to a lesser extent, in higher education in the field of ICT.

It is likely that transnational academic and professional accreditation and recognition will continue to grow, and the international co-ordinating efforts of professional associations will increase the pressure for further co-ordination of quality assurance and accreditation in both vocational and higher education across borders.

6. CONCLUSION AND POLICY ISSUES

Greater international supply of post-secondary education can serve, broadly, two strategic objectives. A "culture-driven" strategy is based on the idea that student exchange is beneficial for both host and sending countries in terms of cultural, social and political values. To a greater or lesser extent, all OECD countries seek to achieve such objectives, and offer public and/or private funded grants to encourage such exchange, and promote regional programmes to facilitate student mobility. More recently, some countries have also been influenced by a "trade-driven" strategy of promoting the export of educational services for economic benefit. Such a strategy is characterised by higher levels of tuition fees for foreign students, by government and institutional marketing and support programmes to attract foreign students, and by the inclusion of trade in educational services in the GATS.

The emergence of a substantial international market for educational services has to a large extent been demand-driven, particularly by students from the rapidly developing countries of North and South-East Asia. There are many different factors behind this growing demand, including capacity constraints in the home country, and the opportunities for broader educational experiences, and more widely recognised qualifications, in mainly high-income and English-speaking countries. Increasing demand for international

education has triggered a number of initiatives by various education providers, whether traditional universities, distance-learning institutions, or private education and training companies. Increasingly, providers are joining together in partnerships to meet demand more effectively.

These developments raise a number of questions for OECD governments in their direct or indirect roles in funding, regulating, monitoring and delivering post-secondary education. They imply a more complex environment with a wider range of education and training providers becoming involved, increased connectivity and interdependence among national education systems, and pressure for greater coherence among the national frameworks of post-secondary education. Moves towards greater coherence are already evident in some regions, for example within the European Higher Education Area.

In particular, three issues – access, funding/regulation, and quality – that are already central to national debates about post-secondary education, now need to be confronted in an international context.

Student access. A key question is the extent to which students are benefiting from the increasing international mobility and trade in educational services. Increasing competition between national and foreign providers potentially creates greater opportunities and flexibility for student choice of post-secondary education. In most developing countries, less than 5% of the population currently has access to post-secondary education. The number who wish to enrol is bound to increase substantially in the coming years as the objective of providing nine years of basic education for all is progressively achieved (UNESCO, 2000).

It is highly unlikely that many developing countries will be able to meet all of this demand in the near future. Initiatives in distance-learning programmes linked with educational infrastructure in other countries may be a cost-effective means of meeting some of the demand. Programmes currently underway in China, India and in other developing countries provide examples of how to widen access to post-secondary education through these means. However, very few e-learning initiatives in higher education have so far been successful, and knowledge about the costs and benefits of these initiatives in developed as well as developing countries is very limited (Tyan, 2002). Yet, e-learning seems bound to grow.

Despite the undoubted contribution of international mobility and transnational provision in opening up more opportunities for students, critics of international competition and trade in post-secondary education emphasise the risks of a growing market-oriented approach to post-secondary education, believing that this would lead to the entry of more for-profit providers and more programmes of questionable quality. Governments have to balance these different points of view.

Funding and regulation. In many countries, post-secondary education institutions need to seek alternative sources of funding as direct government support per student is stable or declining. This funding pressure often means that institutions have to seek new funding sources such as private sector sources of financial support, tuition fees for domestic students, and fee-paying students from abroad. Moreover, new national and/or foreign providers are increasingly meeting the demand for post-secondary education and training. These developments imply that governments need to reflect on their funding and regulatory framework for foreign public and private providers in post-secondary education.

A key choice for governments is whether foreign education providers would be eligible for the same grants, subsidies and tax initiatives as domestic education providers. As noted earlier, even countries that agree to liberalise trade in education through the GATS retain the freedom to determine the conditions under which such market access occurs.

The trends towards greater cross-border provision and consumption of educational services were already well established before the GATS commitments in educational services were initiated in 1995, and much of the trade in educational services takes place outside the GATS framework. Whatever happens in the current round of GATS negotiations, the trends towards greater cross-

border provision and consumption of educational services are bound to continue, stimulated in part by some governments' wishes to diversify and increase the competition within their post-secondary education sector. This, in turn, might encourage more institutional mergers and a concentration of disciplines within institutions in order to create larger and more robust institutions able to attract sufficient numbers of both domestic and international students. Such developments can already be seen in Denmark, Japan and the United Kingdom, for example. Governments can guide such developments by incentive-based funding of mergers and flexible partnerships.

Quality. The quality of internationally traded educational services is a key issue for both enthusiasts and critics of the expansion of these services. A central question is to what extent governments and higher education institutions wish to supplement their national quality assurance initiatives with international ones, and/or to seek other ways of helping students to navigate their way through the new international markets in educational services.

At present, very diverse quality assurance and accreditation mechanisms for higher education are in place in different OECD countries. Almost all current quality assurance models are confined to the educational activities of institutions within national boundaries. These are supplemented by international initiatives such as the UNESCO/Council of Europe Lisbon Convention and the European Bologna process to secure better consumer protection against low-quality programmes and to enhance transparency. The recent Japanese proposal on educational services in the framework of the GATS negotiations raises this issue. However, the trade agreements under the WTO are not mandated to deal directly with international quality assurance issues. The WTO can, however, play a role in increasing the transparency of recognition and licensing arrangements.

It is very unlikely that a comprehensive international quality assurance system could be developed that would substitute for national policies and procedures. Today there are very few mechanisms for international quality assurance in educational services. Even most student mobility programmes and existing schemes of credit recognition and transfer, such as the ECTS in Europe, do not involve any quality control. However, some international procedures for validation, and sometimes even accreditation, of programmes and institutions, have been established by professional organisations for professions such as engineers and accountants, and within the ICT sector. Fuelled by the increasing mobility of professional labour, the importance of such professional accreditation procedures will continue to grow, and will increase pressure to co-ordinate quality assurance and accreditation across borders.

A more co-ordinated international effort in post-secondary quality assurance and accreditation will, to a large extent, depend on agreement from all the stakeholders – from quality assurance and accreditation agencies, professional associations, public and private providers, and education policy makers. So far, there has not been much exchange of ideas or collaboration between these stakeholders at the international level. The new developments in transnational education and e-learning will, however, challenge existing national quality assurance and accreditation agencies and frameworks, thus increasing the pressure to make new efforts internationally.

References

ASCHER, B. (2002), "International dimensions of certification and accreditation: the role of trade agreements", Paper prepared for the Open Forum on ISO/IEC 17024, Accreditation of Personnel Certification Bodies, Washington DC, February.

BENNELL, P. and **PEARCE, T.** (1998), "The internationalisation of higher education: exporting education to developing and transitional economics", Institute of Development Studies, Working Paper, Brighton, UK.

CUNNINGHAM, S., RYAN, Y., STEDMAN, L., TAPSALL, S., BAGDON, S., FLEW, T., and **COALDRAKE, P.** (2000), *The Business of Borderless Education*, Australian Department of Education, Training and Youth Affairs, Canberra.

DENSFORD, L. (1999), "Many CUs under development", *Corporate University Review*, Vol. 7, No. 1.

IDP EDUCATION AUSTRALIA and **AUSTRALIAN EDUCATION INTERNATIONAL** (2002), *Comparative Costs of Higher Education Courses for International Students in Australia, New Zealand, the United Kingdom, Canada and the United States*, Sydney.

KNIGHT, J. (2002), "Trade in higher education services: the implications of GATS", *Observatory on Borderless Higher Education*, *www.obhe.ac.uk/products/reports/pdf/March2002.pdf*.

LARSEN, K., MARTIN J. and **MORRIS, R.** (2002), "Trade in educational services: trends and issues", *The World Economy*, Vol. 25, No. 6, Blackwell Publishing, Oxford, UK, and Boston, USA.

MCBURNIE, G. and **ZIGURAS, C.** (2001), "The regulation of transnational higher education in Southeast Asia : case studies of Hong Kong, Malaysia and Australia", *Higher Education*, Vol. 42, pp. 85-105.

MEISTER, J. (1998), *Corporate Universities: Lessons in Building a World-class Workforce*, McGraw Hill, New York.

OECD (various years), *Education at a Glance: OECD Indicators*, Paris.

OECD (2001), *E-Learning – The Partnership Challenge*, Paris.

OECD (2002a), *Student Mobility Between and Towards OECD Countries – A Comparative Analysis*, Paris.

OECD (2002*b*), GATS: *The Case for Open Services Markets*, Paris.

OECD (2002*c*), "Current commitments under the GATS in educational services", Background document prepared for the OECD/US Forum on Trade in Educational Services, May, Washington D.C.

SAUVÉ, P. (2002), "Trade, education and the GATS : what's in, what's out, what's all the fuss about?", Paper prepared for the OECD/US Forum on Trade in Educational Services, May, Washington D.C.

TYAN, Y. (2002), *Emerging Indicators of Success and Failures in Borderless Higher Education*, The Observatory on Borderless Higher Education, February, London.

UNESCO (2000), *The Dakar Framework for Action. Education for All: Meeting Our Collective Commitments*, Paris.

UNESCO (various years), *Statistical Yearbooks*, Paris.

VAN DAMME, D. (2002), "Trends and models in international quality assurance and accreditation in higher education in relation to trade in education services", Paper prepared for the OECD/US Forum on Trade in Educational Services, May, Washington D.C.

WTO (1998), *Education Services*, 23 September 1998 (S/C/W/49), Geneva.

WTO (2000), A *Review of Statistics on Trade Flows in Services*, 30 October 2000 (S/C/27/Add.1), Geneva.

Data for the Figures

Data for Figures 4.1 and 4.4 are shown on the Figures.

Data for Figure 4.2

Increase of foreign tertiary students in OECD countries, 1980-99 (1990 = 100)

	1980		1990		1999	
	Number	Index	Number	Index	Number	Index
Australia	8 777	30	28 993	100	99 014	342
Austria	11 848	64	18 434	100	29 819	162
Canada	28 443	81	35 187	100	35 543	101
France	110 763	79	139 963	100	130 952	94
Germany	57 423	59	97 985	100	178 195	181
Japan	15 211	39	38 794	100	56 552	146
New Zealand	2 464	76	3 229	100	6 900	214
United Kingdom	56 003	70	80 183	100	232 518	290
United States	311 882	77	407 518	100	451 934	111
OECD average	710 474	71	1 004 522	100	1 477 049	147

Source: UNESCO for 1980 and 1990, except for Japan (Ministry of Education); OECD Education database for 1999.

Data for Figure 4.3

Number of foreign students per domestic student abroad in tertiary education by OECD country, 1995 and 1999

	1995			1999		
	Foreign students	Domestic students abroad	Ratio	Foreign students	Domestic students abroad	Ratio
Australia	81 430	4 435	18.36	99 014	5 169	19.15
Austria	25 175	9 686	2.60	29 819	11 354	2.63
Belgium	34 966	6 333	5.52	36 137	9 400	3.84
Canada	54 712	27 300	2.00	35 543	27 181	1.31
Czech Republic	3 224	2 332	1.38	4 583	3 752	1.22
Denmark	8 313	4 444	1.87	12 315	6 283	1.96
Finland	2 566	3 721	0.69	4 847	9 471	0.51
France	165 350	34 846	4.75	130 952	48 235	2.71
Germany	154 536	40 816	3.79	178 195	51 599	3.45
Greece	m	36 638	m	m	57 825	m
Hungary	6 394	4 098	1.56	8 869	6 313	1.40
Iceland	160	m	m	207	2 433	0.09
Ireland	5 177	12 383	0.42	7 183	19 041	0.38
Italy	24 014	29 698	0.81	23 496	39 295	0.60
Japan	53 511	56 685	0.94	56 552	56 250	1.01
Korea	1 983	61 383	0.03	2 869	62 892	0.05
Luxembourg	m	m	m	652	5 411	0.12
Mexico	m	12 080	m	2 293	13 520	0.17
Netherlands	m	11 870	m	13 619	15 251	0.89
New Zealand	5 883	1 331	4.42	6 900	1 650	4.18
Norway	11 158	6 636	1.68	9 004	11 962	0.75
Poland	5 202	9 835	0.53	5 693	15 101	0.38
Portugal	m	8 158	m	m	m	m
Slovak Republic	m	m	m	m	m	m
Spain	21 403	21 087	1.01	32 954	25 687	1.28
Sweden	m	8 456	m	19 567	13 360	1.46
Switzerland	17 517	7 341	2.39	25 258	8 458	2.99
Turkey	14 719	35 142	0.42	19 816	43 847	0.45
United Kingdom	156 977	23 850	6.58	232 588	22 166	10.49
United States	452 705	23 369	19.37	451 934	30 175	14.98

m: missing data.

Note: "Domestic students abroad" reflects only students studying in OECD countries.

Source: OECD Education database.

Data for Figure 4.5

Distribution of international students enrolled in Australian universities by mode of study, 1996 to 2001 (% of international students)

Year (semester 2)	On-campus in Australia	Distance learning while living in home country	Offshore campus or affiliate of Australian university
1996	75.9	5.9	18.3
1997	72.4	6.3	21.3
1998	69.8	6.2	24.0
1999	67.4	5.2	27.4
2000	63.2	8.5	28.3
2001	63.5	9.0	27.6

Source: IDP Education Australia.

chapter 5
RETHINKING HUMAN CAPITAL

SUMMARY

Investment in human capital is now seen as central to the development of advanced economies and democratic societies. This chapter suggests that there is more to human capital than the more readily measurable – and very important – literacy, numeracy and workplace skills.

Educational attainment and readily measurable skills account for less than half of individual wage differences in OECD countries. Part of the remainder may be explained by a "wider" form of human capital, defined as the characteristics that allow a person to build, manage and deploy his or her skills. These include the ability and motivation to learn, effective job search skills, and personal characteristics that help one work well, as well as the capacity to blend a successful life with a good career.

Individuals need to learn how to manage their long-term goals, both job-related and social, as well as acquiring specific skills for finding work. The development of these characteristics – such as the ability to plan and think ahead – will depend not only on early experience at home, but also on the active role of schools and colleges in nurturing these abilities. Careers education and guidance can be central to this, and needs to support long-term learning strategies, and work with other influences, including those of family and peers.

The wider concept of human capital helps bridge the gap between those who emphasise education's economic mission, and those who emphasise broader social and personal benefits. The chapter proposes policy directions for building wider human capital, and outlines a supporting research and evaluation agenda.

1. INTRODUCTION

The notion of human capital, and its place in policies for education systems and the economy, is under intensive debate. Human capital is increasingly seen as an engine of national economic growth and development. At the same time, the goal of education is to prepare for life as well as for work, and the economic role of education needs to be placed in the context of the development of "whole" individuals – not just their working skills. Issues of measurement and testing present a separate, but related challenge. While many measures of educational outcomes concern knowledge and skills, qualities like creativity and teamworking skills are harder to test and measure, although they are receiving increasing attention both in the workplace and in non-working life. Moral and civic qualities – for example compassion, or the understanding of democratic institutions – are also important potential outcomes of education. In the face of these multiple demands, our understanding of human capital needs to develop and change.

This chapter sets out an approach designed to broaden the way we think about human capital and how it relates to systems of learning and production. Drawing on new and existing evidence, it suggests that, alongside skills that directly enhance productive capacity, a wider set of attributes play an important role in human capital. This "wider human capital" is defined as the capacity to develop, manage and deploy one's own competencies, for example by investing in further learning, by finding a job that suits one's talents and by developing facets of one's character that enhance one's effectiveness at work. The evidence so far available suggests that greater emphasis in educational policy making needs to be given to such attributes, since they play a key part in determining productivity, as well as affecting individual and social well-being.

This chapter may be set in the context of a wide range of other work which is beginning to illustrate the diverse elements which contribute to human capital. This diversity has been well illustrated by the outcome of the OECD exercise entitled "Definition and Selection of Competencies" in which a number of OECD countries collaborated to identify competencies for life (DeSeCo, 2001).

Other work has looked, for example, at the non-economic outcomes of education and training, at the role of motivational traits in the labour market, and at more complex intellectual capacities like creativity and problem-solving. One implication of the analysis presented here, alongside these new strands in the human capital literature, is that a better understanding of how a range of human attributes contribute to economic output leads to a better understanding of the wider social, personal and cultural benefits of education and training. The first part of this chapter – in Sections 2 and 3 – therefore explores human capital largely from the economic perspective of monetary returns. Later sections pursue the implications for the wider benefits of education and training.

The following analysis uses the OECD's broad definition of human capital, as:

The knowledge, skills, competencies and attributes embodied in individuals that facilitate the creation of personal, social and economic well-being (OECD, 2001a).

As illustrated in Figure 5.1, these attributes are potentially derived not only from formal education and training, but also from a person's background, experiences and innate qualities. They can have a bearing not only on individual wages and job prospects, but also on overall productivity, and on well-being. Just as different strands of human capital may have different origins, they may also have different kinds of impact. For example, the capacities necessary for a rewarding private life are unlikely to be identical to the interpersonal skills required in the work place, even though there may be a large overlap.

Policy makers need to improve their understanding of which forms of human capital derive from various influences and what are their different impacts. The part played by education compared to other influences and innate qualities, is of great significance. To what extent can education overcome disadvantages associated with a poor family background, and to which aspects of human capital can education make the greatest contribution?

This chapter makes a start, first of all by considering, in Section 2, how different forms of human capital may affect earnings. The evidence here

| Figure 5.1 | Human capital – sources, aspects and outcomes |

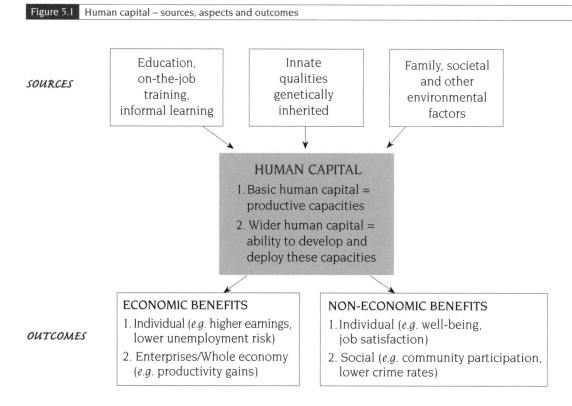

indicates that the narrower forms of human capital that are more susceptible to measurement tell only part of the story. Section 3 therefore considers the role of wider forms of human capital – in particular, people's ability to develop, manage and deploy their own skills – in relation to individual economic gain as well as to wider economic and social benefits. It suggests that, while some people help improve the operation of labour and skills markets by managing their human capital well, others lack the attributes that would lead them to invest in education and skills in the first place. Section 4 looks more specifically at the significance for education systems of the capacity to manage one's own learning, for which a measure has been developed at the school level. Section 5 considers what can be done at the policy level to develop wider forms of human capital, in the context of the multiple sources of human capital shown at the top of the diagram in Figure 5.1. Section 6 concludes by pointing to some of the new priorities that this implies for education systems, and to how further research can improve our understanding of the way in which different forms of human capital are developed and applied.

2. HOW HUMAN CAPITAL AFFECTS EARNINGS: THE EVIDENCE

2.1 Cognitive skills and education as determinants of earnings

The International Adult Literacy Survey (IALS) tested the literacy and numeracy skills of adults in a number of countries in the mid-1990s and is the main internationally comparable source of data on earnings in relation to direct measures of cognitive skill (OECD, 2000). The survey also asked about other factors that can contribute to human capital and earnings, including educational background, work experience and social background.

About 40% of individual variation in earnings is explicable through IALS measures such as educational qualifications, literacy and work experience, combined with the background factors of gender, language and parents' education levels. Around half the variation in earnings was explained for Canada, the United Kingdom and Chile, but only about a quarter for Finland and Poland. In most cases, education had more explanatory power

Box 5.1 Human capital and the determination of earnings in the labour market

Under the idealised circumstances of what economists call "perfect competition" wages are entirely determined by worker productivity at the margin. An employer will go on employing more workers until, through a process of diminishing returns, the extra output contributed by the last worker employed (productivity at the margin) falls until it is just equal to the cost of employing that worker.

The added value of an individual's skill, and its reward, will also depend on whether that skill is in short supply. In another idealised market – this time in human capital investment – wage rewards from skills will tend to equate with the costs of acquiring those skills. This is because rewards over and above such costs will encourage more investment in that skill (through education and training). Such investment will increase the supply of that skill, which will in turn lower its wage reward until it is equal to the costs of acquiring the skill (removing the "extra" incentive for acquiring the skill).

The upshot, if both these markets were working perfectly, is that wages would be equivalent to productivity at the margin, and the wage benefits associated with particular skills would be equivalent to the cost of acquiring those skills. Moreover, in these perfect markets, people would reap no rewards from "wise" decisions about job choice or human capital investment, because true bargains, in the sense of choices which yield unusually large returns, do not exist in the long run. Others in the market recognise such opportunities, raising their price until they are no longer bargains.

In practice, neither market bears much resemblance to these idealised versions. First, a very large range of factors, other than productivity, affect wages. Wages vary by firm size, even within the same industry, with larger firms generally paying higher wages. Workers do not always manage to find the job which will make best use of their skills. Employer preferences, including discrimination, will bias wages. Even when employers do seek to match wages to productivity the match may be weak, because their measures of individual employee productivity may be poor, and institutional constraints on wage-bargaining mean that the scope for employers to match wages to individual human capital is generally limited. Wages will also reflect the relative attractiveness of different types of work to workers and variations in attitudes to risk. For example, those who place a high value on employment security may accept lower wages in return for a secure job (Raudenbusch and Kasim, 1998).

Modern labour economics also suggests that employers may often have incentives to pay "efficiency" wages (higher than labour productivity at the margin). Such wage levels reduce costly staff turnover and monitoring costs by giving staff an incentive to stay in jobs and not to risk the sack through shirking.

Human capital investment is also less neat than in the idealised model. The wage rewards for particular skills (like ICT skills) can be volatile, with long time lags before additional training can adjust the stock to meet demand. Risk again plays a part, since profitable but risky forms of human capital investment may be avoided by those who shun risk. Student ignorance of course contents and career outcomes sometimes leads to poor course choices, and choice is in any case constrained by institutional factors in educational systems. Many non-economic incentives also bear on course choice – for example, some courses are more enjoyable than others – increasing the supply of the skills acquired, and depressing the associated wage returns. For all these reasons, the wage rewards from a skill will not necessarily be commensurate with the cost of acquiring that skill, or the time taken to do so.

than literacy (Denny *et al.*, 2000; Boudard, 2001). Analysis of the survey results for the United States, Canada, the Netherlands, Sweden and Switzerland shows that length of education and literacy skills are closely associated, but that they each have a separate, roughly equal, effect (Blau and Kahn, 2001). US studies of earnings returns to education and measured cognitive skills suggest that the latter account for only about 20-25% of the contribution of years of education to wages (Bowles *et al.*, 2001*b*).

Overall, these findings suggest that earnings prospects are improved by:

– more years in education;

– skills that do not always come from more education, but from other sources; and

– an important set of factors that are not quantified by the measures set out above.

In these studies, the measure of education is limited, whilst those for cognitive skills are narrow. The usual measure of education – the number of years enrolled – takes no account of wide variations in the quality of provision. The cognitive skill measures are also typically based on literacy and numeracy skills measured in pencil-and-paper tests, which have limited power to assess aspects such as lateral thinking and creativity. Nor is there any direct measure of vocational skill – for example, knowledge of electric circuitry for an electrician.

Of the remaining 60% of variation in earnings which is unexplained by the available human capital measures in IALS, how much is due to other, unmeasured, human capital factors, and how much by other factors? Clearly not all earnings variation is due to human capital. People vary in the extent to which they trade off earnings against other job factors, such as job satisfaction and working hours, and measurement error and plain luck cause further variation. Moreover, the link between human capital and earnings is not straightforward. In the textbook world of perfectly operating markets, individual earnings would be determined entirely by each person's productive capacity and the level of individual investment in productive capacity. In practice, however, a number of complicating issues mean that many other factors are involved (see Box 5.1). Some of these factors – like discrimina-

tion on grounds of race and gender, or sudden, technology-induced changes in the demand for particular skills – are largely beyond the control of the individual wage earner. Others will not be. The relationship pictured in Figure 5.1 between human capital and its economic benefits is therefore far from simple.

2.2 Personal characteristics that influence earnings

Some recent studies suggest that part of the "missing" influence on earnings comes from motivation and other personal characteristics which are associated with higher average earnings (see Box 5.2). In a world of perfect information, the link between performance-enhancing personality traits and wages would be an indirect one: directly, employers would observe and reward the higher output of those with such traits. However, in practice, employers make recruitment decisions on the basis of limited information, may monitor individual productivity imperfectly and often face heavy costs if they decide to shed labour. This is one reason why employers place a direct value on attributes like trustworthiness, self-discipline or team-working capacity.

Other characteristics may also enhance earnings, without necessarily being attractive to employers. Entrepreneurial individuals may search out job opportunities where, at least temporarily, the supply of labour has not kept up with demand and extra earnings are therefore available (Bowles *et al.*, 2001*b*). An obvious corollary is the possibility of identifying and investing in a skill for which there is (temporarily) excess demand. These considerations suggest the need for a widening of the concept of human capital, along the lines developed in the following section.

3. A WIDER CONCEPTION OF HUMAN CAPITAL

3.1 Managing one's own productive capabilities

The evidence reviewed above shows that some personal characteristics that influence earnings are not related to direct productive abilities, but to people's dispositions and the way they behave. This observation may be linked to a more fundamental point. Human capital differs from physical capital in that people manage themselves whereas machines, as a rule, do not. People manage themselves by

Box 5.2 **Personality and motivational characteristics, earnings and job performance**

There is growing evidence from studies undertaken in the United States that many personality characteristics and motivational traits affect earnings. Much of the literature is reviewed in Bowles *et al.* (2001*b*). Direct evidence emerges from studies like those by Cawley *et al.* (2001) who show that socialisation skills acquired at school are related to earnings – these include "the self-discipline to follow the rules, to show up at school on time, and not to abuse drugs or alcohol". Such skills help to drive later educational attainment and earnings. A study of a rather broader range of personality characteristics by Kuhn and Weinberger (2001) shows that leadership qualities, alongside sociability, self-confidence and other personality measures all have independent positive effects on earnings.

There is also evidence linking job performance to personal attributes. Pencil-and-paper personality tests are commonly used in personnel selection, testing for characteristics seen as desirable such as conscientiousness, openness to experience, extraversion, agreeableness, and undesirable characteristics such as neuroticism. The value of such tests depends on two assumptions: that such characteristics can be accurately determined through the tests and that they are relevant to subsequent job performance. Evaluations of the effectiveness of such tests in predicting subsequent job performance have tested the degree to which the two assumptions are jointly valid.

In these evaluations, job performance is commonly measured either through supervisor assessments or through outcomes such as promotions, wages and productivity. While individual results have been mixed, reviews of research in this field show positive results. One review shows that openness to experience, agreeableness and (negatively) neuroticism are particularly important. Unsurprisingly, personality tests are most effective at predicting performance when they are based on an analysis of the personality requirements in a particular job (Tett and Jackson, 1991).

Employers commonly cite personality and motivational traits as very important selection criteria in recruitment. A recent survey in the United States by the National Association of Colleges and Employers (NACE, 2000) found that employers' five most highly-valued personal qualities, in order, were: communications skills; motivation/initiative; team-working skills; leadership skills; and academic achievement.

attempting to make the best use of their existing skills in the labour market, and by sustaining and developing those skills over time. Given turbulence, uncertainty and gaps in labour markets and in markets for human capital investment, individuals can increase their earnings by managing their own productive skills wisely. This could involve spotting a job where one's skills would be best employed, or developing a skill that is in short supply.

Such "wider" forms of human capital facilitate efficient identification and acquisition of skills in short supply, and efficient use of existing skills. They therefore

do more than just give individual advantage; they contribute to overall economic output, and overall well-being, by putting the right people with the right skills in the right place in the economy.

A fuller conception of human capital could therefore comprise:

Basic human capital

– Productive capacities and characteristics (like carpentry skills, physical strength, creativity, communication ability). These can be thought of as "skills", broadly defined.

Wider human capital

– Characteristics that allow a person to build, manage and deploy basic human capital.

These include:

(i) The ability to acquire and develop skills. This includes the ability to learn, to identify one's learning needs and to manage one's learning activity.

(ii) The ability to find the best place to utilise these skills. This includes career planning, job search skills, and the ability to blend working and personal objectives.

(iii) Personal characteristics (like trustworthiness) which make people more attractive as employees, because they are more likely to deploy their skills productively. Motivational characteristics are likely to be central.

Some general skills and characteristics apply across these boundaries: general intelligence helps people to be good at particular jobs and to manage their own careers; self-discipline adds to productive capacity and supports learning skills. Other attributes and skills increase individual earnings but not output, and should not therefore be regarded as genuine human capital. Race and gender, under conditions of discrimination, fall into this category.

The range of competencies involved in wider human capital is not only relevant to choosing courses and finding jobs in the open market, but also to *internal* labour markets within enterprises – particularly in the case of large firms. Within organisations, individuals can advance their careers not only by proving themselves to be good at particular jobs, but also by actively learning on the job, and by securing the career moves and training which will advance their careers. Moreover, these competencies will also be attractive to employers since workers with these skills will play an active and creative part in the development of the organisation's skill base. This is particularly likely in enterprises subject to rapid innovation, where central planning of human capital requirements may be too inflexible. Employers may be willing to recognise and reward these competencies directly because some of the economic benefits arising from them will accrue to the enterprise, as well as to the individual.

Effective management of one's career involves more than simply maximising earnings. It is also about ensuring job satisfaction, and finding a career which can be effectively woven into the other demands on one's life, including private, family and community life. The ability to pursue these other concerns is very much part of human capital.

One motivational characteristic which may play a particularly important role is the willingness to trade current for future benefits – "future-directedness" (sometimes called "time preference" by economists). Future-directed individuals tend to take career planning more seriously and to make human capital investments which typically involve a trade off between current and future benefits. Bowles *et al.* (2001*a*) identify this characteristic as being attractive to employers because it increases the incentive for employees to avoid being caught shirking and hence lose their jobs. One might add that it will also increase the incentive to develop skills on the job, and to comply with instructions in the hope of future preferment. The characteristic of future-directedness therefore both supports the effective career planning which leads to higher earnings, and may increase earnings directly.

Writers on career guidance have arrived at a similar notion of self-management as part of human capital. The purpose of career education and guidance has been defined as that of enabling "pupils to develop the skills, attitudes and knowledge which will help them to make and implement career decisions, and so to manage their progression in learning and work throughout their lives" (Killeen *et al.*, 1999). It has been argued that the value of this activity includes that of reducing the market "imperfections" arising from issues like job mismatch or information failures in human capital investment, while also taking account of wider and non-economic objectives, including job satisfaction (Watts, 1999).

Twelve OECD countries have recently identified the key competencies they believed were important in the different spheres of working, family and community life (DeSeCo, 2001). Virtually all countries identified "learning competence/lifelong learning" and "self-competence/self-management" as important. The latter involved "selecting goals for oneself, planning and implementing self-defined goals, coping with obstacles and redefining one's goals". These two domains both relate to wider human capital.

3.2 Can wider human capital help explain the outcomes of education?

This wider conception of human capital may help to explain some of the broader (non-economic) benefits of education. For example, OECD (2001a) shows that additional full-time education is associated with a reduced risk of smoking, better well-being, lower criminal involvement, and higher participation in community groups. Cognitive skills in isolation cannot easily explain these outcomes. Cognitive recognition of the well-advertised health risks of smoking, for example, requires no more than basic education. Conversely, a "future-directed" willingness to trade current pleasures for future health benefits, combined with self-discipline, is relevant to smoking behaviour. Those involved in crime have also often been identified as impulsive and without concern for the future (Gottfredson and Hirschi, 1990). Participation in civic life requires cognitive skills, but it also requires the disposition to see oneself as a "stakeholder" in society, a disposition with a "future-directed" dimension (Glaeser et al., 2000). Collectively, these non-cognitive characteristics help to explain the non-monetary benefits of education. One implication is that achieving these benefits requires a broad-based education rather than one narrowly focused on cognitive skills.

The economic returns to individuals from particular courses of education and training vary considerably among individuals (Carneiro et al., 2001). Prior ability and qualifications affect returns, and there is some evidence that, for this reason, enterprise training is concentrated on those who already have good initial levels of educational attainment (OECD, 1999), recognising that qualifications may be used by employers as a screening device to identify those with training potential. Successful learning not only requires prior cognitive skills such as literacy and numeracy: it also requires the motivation to learn, and the capacity to direct one's own learning, an understanding of

how the qualification and associated skill can be applied, and knowledge of how to "sell" the skill to employers. One reason for poor returns from particular learner-course combinations may therefore be a lack of these wider forms of human capital – a lack which is hard to identify in advance. Conversely the returns from such skills include the capacity to reap higher returns from making better use of one's human capital investment. This benefit may be very large, given that research has demonstrated high returns from upper secondary and tertiary education, and a wide variation around the average (Carneiro et al., 2001; Blöndal et al., 2002).

4. TOWARDS MEASUREMENT: THE LEARNING PROCESS

Not all of these wider forms of human capital can readily be measured, but there are some useful indicators. Self-management of learning includes both "macro" decisions about, for example, whether to enter tertiary education, and "micro" decisions about, for example, study strategies in support of learning objectives. The recent Programme for International Student Assessment (PISA) study of the competencies of 15-year olds in a number of OECD and non-OECD countries has cast new light on motivation and learning and the significance of self-directed learning (OECD, 2001b). (While many other personal attributes are of course also relevant to learning, it is these ones which have now been successfully measured.)

Within countries, students reporting a greater interest in reading achieved substantially better results in tests of reading literacy than those with less interest, and students reporting a greater than average interest in mathematics achieved somewhat better results in tests of numerical reasoning.[1] Moreover, those who said they like school also tended to achieve better results. These findings do not demonstrate causation: they could indicate that motivation leads to better performance, that better performance enhances motivation, or that some underlying factor enhances both motivation and performance. Perhaps the most plausible explanation is that motivation and performance are mutually reinforcing.

---

1. These results from PISA are discussed in more detail in Chapter 2.

In the PISA project, one aspect of students' capacity to manage their own learning was assessed by asking students how often they consider what they need to learn, look for additional required information, and check that they have remembered the most important things. Within each country, students who used such strategies more frequently tended to perform better on the reading scale, other factors being equal. The significance of this behaviour is not only that it contributes to school learning, but that it is a tool that can be used throughout life. In recognition of this, the first PISA report suggested that "schools may need to give more explicit attention to allowing students to manage and control their learning" (OECD, 2001*b*).

This view is reinforced by evidence that, for many adults with poor basic cognitive skills, failure to recognise their own human capital deficiencies is an underlying problem – and itself a shortfall in wider human capital. Among those performing at the lowest Level 1 of the prose literacy scale in the International Adult Literacy Survey, roughly the same number of people claim their reading skills are "excellent" (13%) as "poor" (11%). Of those who say that they are not at all limited by their reading skills in their opportunities for promotion or mobility at work, 40% are at Levels 1 and 2. Such findings point to the possibility that one of the main barriers to advancement for those with the weakest skills could be the way they assess and manage their own skills.

5. CONTEXTS FOR POLICY INTERVENTION

This section considers the roles of school, family and social environments in the development of wider forms of human capital (see Figure 5.1) – recognising that some of these environments are easier than others to influence by policy measures. The overall conclusion, however, is that recognition of the importance of wider forms of human capital implies a broadened public policy agenda to help build such capital.

5.1 The influence of schools

It is well established that the number of years an individual spends in education is correlated with subsequent earnings. A traditional debate surrounds the question of whether this is to be interpreted as education promoting cognitive skills which increase earnings, or whether those with higher intellectual ability at the outset tend to stay longer in education and to have higher earnings. Recent research using longitudinal data sets and controlling for prior cognitive ability has shown that most of the earnings benefits reflect genuine increases in productivity driven by education (see Bedard, 2001; Harmon and Walker, 2001).

A wider conception of human capital gives a new twist to the story. Conceivably, greater career-planning skills and dispositions may lead to both a) longer time spent in education, and b) higher earnings. However such career-planning skills may be the effect as well as the cause of time spent in education. Education may foster relevant motivational characteristics, career-planning and job-search skills, and these may in turn contribute to higher earnings. Unfortunately, few data sets contain information about such characteristics, and thus on how successful schools may be in enhancing them. There is some positive evidence to suggest that schooling has an influence on various motivational characteristics, but it remains patchy (Bowles *et al.*, 2001*b*). Kuhn and Weinberger (2001) show that at least one type of broader ability – leadership skills – can be encouraged by offering opportunities for it to develop in the school setting. There is also evidence that career guidance in schools can contribute to developing career-planning skills (see Section 5.3).

5.2 The influence of parents

In many OECD countries, young people whose parents have completed some tertiary education are about twice as likely to participate in tertiary education as those whose parents lack upper secondary qualifications. Well-educated parents tend to be more affluent, encouraging their children, for example, to go to university through financial support. However, parental education may also affect the education of children more directly. First, education increases the cognitive skills and knowledge of parents, and therefore supports their capacity to explain things to their children and act as informal teachers. Second, better educated parents may pass on some wider aspects of human capital, both through example and through direct encouragement. Such aspects could include a commitment to learning and a familiarity with learning strategies, a recognition of the labour market value of qualifications, and an understanding of how to best exploit that value.

There is some evidence that this second kind of influence may be important. Evidence from the United States shows that it is not possible to explain the persistence of intergenerational inequality simply by reference to the advantages of wealth or the inheritance or transmission of cognitive skills – suggesting that other personality characteristics passed from parent to child must also be important (Bowles *et al.*, 2001*b*). PISA shows that parental education plays a relatively modest role in determining cognitive skills at age 15,[2] particularly when set against the large absolute differences in subsequent rates of participation in tertiary education. One UK research study shows that parental interest in the schooling of children has a sustained impact, other things being equal, not only on the attainment of post-compulsory qualifications but also on the impact of that qualification on subsequent earnings (Dearden, 1998). The implication is that parental expectations may affect their children's motivation to stay in education. Tertiary students will very often be giving up current earning and spending opportunities in order to invest in their education and a future stream of benefits from that education – other things equal, they are likely therefore to be more future-directed. As Bowles *et al.* (2001*a*) argue, such a characteristic is likely to appeal to employers, irrespective of productive capacity. This result suggests that the contribution of parents may be some degree of future-directedness which is passed on to the child, perhaps combined with the ability to fully exploit their human capital in the labour market.

Other considerations support this view. While a teacher may be able to supply the cognitive explanations that a parent cannot, and some guidance on learning strategies, teachers face much greater challenges in seeking to motivate children and support them in the complex career decisions they need to make. The important role played by parents in this area underlines the significance of attempts by schools to work more closely with parents to help motivate and guide their children.

5.3 The social context and career guidance

Alongside parents, other family members, colleagues and friends play a role in career planning. What matters to the individual is not simply a wide circle of family and friends, but also that the people involved are trusted and well informed about career and educational opportunities. Within organisations, while technical skills may be acquired by formal training, identification of career-enhancing opportunities may depend much more on informal networking. In line with this view, a number of studies have shown that the acquisition of human capital is linked to access to social capital – in the sense of informal networks of trusted social contacts (OECD, 2001*a*). Such access will depend on individual social skills, as well as the existence of networks. Career management skills may go a long way to explaining this link.

Evidence of the potential for positive interventions comes from research on career guidance – the formal provision of information and advice to individuals on educational and career options. Guidance can be delivered by a range of methods, including one-to-one, group sessions, telephone and e-mail. Public provision is most commonly based in education institutions and the public employment service, but can also be based in community settings. Countries typically provide services in all of these settings, but the mix can vary widely (Watts, 1996).

Potentially, the individual benefits of guidance include better learning strategies and career decisions, and greater satisfaction with life. The collective benefits could include better targeted human capital investment and better matching of skills and jobs – and therefore higher output. Recent reviews (Killeen, 1996; Watts, 1999), mainly based on US and UK experiences, provide some positive evidence of short- and medium-term benefits, such that guidance:

---

2. Other factors held constant, each additional year of parental education is associated with an average increase of about 5 points across OECD countries in attainment on the combined reading literacy scale (OECD, 2001*b*). To put this figure in context, the bottom quarter of the student population was, in the average OECD country, 65 points or more below the mean student score.

– can promote positive attitudinal change, including greater interest in education and training and greater motivation to seek employment;

– has a number of positive effects on learning outcomes, including better decision-making skills and awareness of opportunities;

– may encourage participation in formal and informal education and training; and

– yields potential economic benefits in the form of the capacity to find satisfying jobs.

At the same time, many of the longer-term outcomes of career guidance are more difficult to pin down – because of the need for difficult and costly follow-up studies over a number of years.

6. IMPLICATIONS FOR POLICY AND RESEARCH

This chapter has two main conclusions. First, the skills and other characteristics involved in managing one's own human capital – including career planning, self-directed learning and job-search skills – play an important part in delivering both the economic and non-economic benefits of human capital. Second, while family and social environment play a strong role in the development of this wider form of human capital, and some motivational characteristics are difficult to influence, practical initiatives, such as effective support for self-directed learning strategies at school, and career guidance interventions, can encourage the development of such skills and characteristics.

The chapter opened by pointing to the need to integrate the economic and non-economic functions of education, against the background of debate between those who emphasise the economic mission of education and those emphasising the broader social and personal benefits. The widening of the concept of human capital set out in this chapter helps us to bridge this gap. On the one hand, it provides a more subtle understanding of how human capital supports economic output. Output and growth depend not only on direct productive capacities, but also on the ability to manage, develop and apply those capacities. On the other hand, the idea humanises our understanding

of human capital, by representing individuals as empowered managers of their own capital, responsible for its development through learning. It also recognises non-economic outcomes, and the societal dimensions of individual decision making about education, jobs and careers.

A number of policy implications stand out.

– First, governments might usefully *give greater emphasis to the capacity to manage one's own education and career* as a formal goal of education and training. While specific skills may become outdated, this capacity will remain of significance throughout life, supporting lifelong learning and career development. By its very nature, it embraces both economic returns and the wider, indirect benefits to be gained from different forms of education, training and employment. The PISA results have already demonstrated the importance of developing effective strategies to manage one's own learning and such skills may be of increasing importance in the face of developments in ICT-based learning. Schools might also do more to teach pupils about how to choose future courses, and how to search for and obtain jobs which are both satisfying and well-paid. Some very specific skills – such as interview technique and CV preparation – can be readily taught. A diverse set of characteristics and competencies are involved in the capacity to manage one's own career, and more formal and informal recognition of this wider range of competencies in curricula and qualification frameworks should help to entrench their acceptance alongside other more traditionally recognised skills.

– Second, *the role of formal career guidance needs to be broadened*. In particular, the traditional approach of individual guidance for young people towards the end of schooling is not enough. For young people, work experience schemes and community-based projects aimed at researching career opportunities represent promising options. Guidance may also need to be supplemented by relevant training – for example in job-search skills. For adults, guidance needs to be accessible to those in work, the unemployed and those of working age who are not in the labour force. Delivery of guidance therefore might take place in the community, in the workplace and in educational institutions.

– Third, policies in this area need to *take account of the role played by families and peer groups* in key career-planning decisions. School-based teaching needs to build on and strengthen the social context of the individual learner's access to social capital, recognising the research evidence that parents and peers play important roles in developing motivation in the individual, and in supporting both learning and career planning. At the simplest level, parents could become more involved in their children's education, particularly at school. More challengingly, schools could work more closely with parents to enhance their skills in motivating and guiding their children, reaching out, in particular, to disadvantaged families. This would open up the possibility of using parental understanding of career options and planning to support and develop that of the child, and may help to foster a role for the parent, not only in self-directed learning at school, but also in subsequent career decisions (see OECD, 1997). Some useful impact on parents' own career decision-making is also possible.

– Finally, a question arises of how and if *education might seek to encourage desired motivational characteristics*, in addition to cognitive skills. Motivation cannot be created out of nothing, but an educational institution can act to encourage behaviour based on desirable motives, and discourage others.

Data on wider human capital are currently limited, and research is at an early stage. Policy development therefore should be cautious, and needs to go hand-in-hand with further research and data collection. Practical initiatives, such as those outlined above, need to be piloted and evaluated. Follow-up studies will be necessary to see if interventions have fostered competencies, and to see if those competencies have had a valuable impact. Such targeted evaluations will need to be underpinned by a broader research programme on the benefits from wider human capital. Both policy and research issues will need to be addressed in the OECD's own programme of work.

More generally, while there is an emerging literature on personality characteristics and their effect on earnings, there are few sources on competencies such as career planning, job-search skills and associated motivational characteristics. Measuring such skills would be challenging, but certainly not impossible, and could be pursued at two levels. At a general level, broad traits such as "future-directedness" could be measured alongside education and earnings, to explore the extent to which they might explain variations in earnings. Any new survey of adult skills could usefully address this issue, both by exploring learning strategies and by collecting information on factors such as course choice, career planning and "future-directedness". At a more specific level, measurement might be targeted at the labour market relevance of particular teachable skills – for example, one could explore whether skills in Internet searches and access to a computer are related to appropriate choices of courses in further and higher education.

The time dimension is central to wider human capital, concerned as it is with the development over time of learning and career paths. Longitudinal studies would be particularly well-suited to identifying the value of career management skills, and the long-term economic and non-economic benefits.

Current efforts in PISA, and elsewhere, to understand the relationship between interest in learning, strategies to direct learning and the acquisition of cognitive skills, need to be pursued. One policy question on which research might cast light is whether there are key points of intervention – for example, different styles of teaching designed to engage disaffected adolescents – which might lead to a virtuous circle of motivation and learning. A better understanding is needed of the scope of education to encourage positive attitudes and motivation, and about the methods that work and those that do not.

References

BEDARD, K. (2001), "Human capital versus signalling models: university access and high school dropouts", *Journal of Political Economy*, Vol. 109.

BLAU, F. and **KAHN, L.** (2001), *Do Cognitive Test Scores Explain Higher US Wage Inequality?*, NBER Working Paper 8210, Cambridge, MA.

BLÖNDAL, S., FIELD, S. and **GIROUARD, N.** (2002), "Investment in human capital through upper-secondary and tertiary education", *Economic Studies*, No. 34, pp. 41-89, OECD, Paris.

BOUDARD, E. (2001), *Literacy Proficiency, Earnings and Recurrent Training: A Ten Country Comparative Study*, Institute of International Education, Stockholm.

BOWLES, S., GINTIS, H. and **OSBORNE, M.** (2001a), "Incentive-enhancing preferences: personality, behaviour and earnings", *American Economic Review*, Vol. 91, No. 2, pp. 155-158.

BOWLES, S., GINTIS, H. and **OSBORNE, M.** (2001b), "The determinants of earnings: a behavioural approach", *Journal of Economic Literature*, Vol. 39, pp. 1137-1176.

CARNEIRO, P., HANSEN, K. and **HECKMAN, J.** (2001), *Educational Attainment and Labor Market Outcomes: estimating distributions of the returns to educational interventions*, Office of Labour Market Evaluation, presented at the conference "What are the effects of active labour market policy?".

CAWLEY, J., HECKMAN, J. and **VYTLACIL, E.** (2001), "Three observations on wages and measured cognitive ability", *Labour Economics*, Vol. 8, pp. 419-442.

DEARDEN, L. (1998), *Ability, Families, Education and Earnings in Britain*, Institute for Fiscal Studies, London.

DENNY, K., HARMON, C. and **REDMOND, S.** (2000), *Functional Literacy, Educational Attainment and Earnings: Evidence from the International Adult Literacy Survey*, Institute for Fiscal Studies, Dublin.

DESECO (2001), *Country Contribution Process: Summary and Country Reports*, DeSeCo, Geneva.

GLAESER, E., LAIBSON, D. and **SACERDOTE, B.** (2000), *The Economic Approach to Social Capital*, National Bureau of Economic Research Working Paper 7728.

GOTTFREDSON, M. and **HIRSCHI, T.** (1990), *A General Theory of Crime*, Stanford University Press, Stanford.

HARMON, C. and **WALKER, I.** (2001), *The Return to Education: A Review of Evidence, Issues and Deficiencies in the Literature*, Department for Education and Employment, Research Report 254, London.

KILLEEN, J. (1996), "The social context of guidance", in A. Watts, B. Law, J. Killeen, J. Kidd and R. Hawthorn (eds.), *Rethinking Careers Education and Guidance: Theory, Policy and Practice*, Routledge, London.

KILLEEN, J., SAMMONS, P. and **WATTS, A.** (1999), *Careers Work and School Effectiveness*, NICEC Briefing Paper, National Institute for Careers Education and Counselling, Cambridge.

KUHN, P. and **WEINBERGER, C.** (2001), *Leadership Skills and Wages*, University of California at Santa Barbara working paper No. #2-02, University of California, Santa Barbara.

NATIONAL ASSOCIATION OF COLLEGES AND EMPLOYERS (2000), *Ideal Candidate Has Top-Notch Interpersonal Skills, Say Employers*, National Association of Colleges and Employers Newsletter, January 18.

OECD (1997), *Parents as Partners in Schooling*, Paris.

OECD (1999), "The training of adult workers in OECD countries: measurement and analysis", *Employment Outlook*, pp. 133-176, Paris.

OECD (2000), *Literacy in the Information Age*, Paris.

OECD (2001a), *The Well-Being of Nations: The Role of Human and Social Capital*, Paris.

OECD (2001b), *Knowledge and Skills for Life: First results from PISA 2000*, Paris.

RAUDENBUSCH, S. and **KASIM, R.** (1998), "Cognitive skill and economic inequality: findings from the National Adult Literacy Survey", *Harvard Educational Review*, Vol. 68, No. 1.

TETT, R. and **JACKSON, D.** (1991), "Personality measures as predictors of job performance: a meta-analytic review", *Personnel Psychology*, No. 44.

WATTS, A. (1996), "International perspectives", in A. Watts, B. Law, J. Killeen, J. Kidd and R. Hawthorn (eds.), *Rethinking Careers Education and Guidance: Theory, Policy and Practice*, Routledge, London, pp. 366-379.

WATTS, A. (1999), "The economic and social benefits of career guidance", *Educational and Vocational Guidance*, No. 63, pp. 12-19.

EDUCATION POLICY ANALYSIS
Purposes and Previous Editions

The Education Policy Analysis series was launched by the OECD in 1996. It forms part of the work programme of the OECD Education Committee, and responds to the policy priorities established by OECD Education Ministers. The series is prepared by the Education and Training Division of the OECD Directorate for Education.

Purposes

The main purposes of Education Policy Analysis are:

- To assist education policy-makers and others concerned with education policy to make better decisions by drawing on international and comparative work;

- To draw out the key insights and policy implications arising from OECD education activities, international data and indicators, and related studies; and

- To present findings, analyses and discussion in a succinct and accessible form.

Education Policy Analysis is produced annually (except in 2000, when a special edition was being prepared for the 2001 OECD Education Ministerial meeting).

Contents of the Previous Editions

ALSO AVAILABLE

Education at a Glance: OECD Indicators 2002 (2002)

Adult Learning: Rhetoric versus Policy Realities (2002)

Understanding the Brain: Towards a New Learning Science (2002)

The Well-being of Nations: The Role of Human and Social Capital (2001)

What Works in Innovation in Education: New School Management Approaches (2001)

E-Learning: The Partnership Challenge (2001)

Starting Strong: Early Childhood Education and Care (2001)

Current Issues in Chinese Higher Education (2001)

Schooling for Tomorrow: What Schools for the Future (2001)

Learning to Change: ICT in Schools (2001)

Economics and Finance of Lifelong Learning (2001)

Programme for International Student Assessment (PISA):

PISA 2000 Technical Report (2002)

Manual for the PISA 2000 Database (2002)

Sample Taks from the PISA 2000 Assessment: Reading, Mathematical and Scientific Literacy (2002)

Knowledge and Skills for Life: First Results from PISA 2000 (2001)

Reviews of National Policies for Education

Reviews of National Policies for Education: Polytechnic Education in Finland (2002)

Reviews of National Policies for Education: Lifelong Learning in Norway (2002)

Reviews of National Policies for Education: Lithuania (2002)

Reviews of National Policies for Education: Estonia (2001)

Reviews of National Policies for Education: Latvia (2001)

OECD PUBLICATIONS, 2, rue André-Pascal, 75775 PARIS CEDEX 16
PRINTED IN FRANCE
(96 2002 04 1 P) ISBN 92-64-19930-6 – No. 52737 2002